# The New Social Question

# NEW FRENCH THOUGHT

Series Editors
*Thomas Pavel and Mark Lilla*

*Pierre Rosanvallon*

# The New Social Question

## RETHINKING THE WELFARE STATE

*Translated by Barbara Harshav*

*With a Foreword by Nathan Glazer*

 **NEW FRENCH THOUGHT**

PRINCETON UNIVERSITY PRESS · PRINCETON, NEW JERSEY

Translated from the French edition of Pierre Rosanvallon's *La nouvelle question sociale: Repenser l'Etat-providence* (Paris: Seuil, 1995)

*Library of Congress Cataloging-in-Publication Data*

Rosanvallon, Pierre, 1948– .
[Nouvelle question sociale. English]
The new social question : rethinking the welfare state / Pierre Rosanvallon ; translated by Barbara Harshav ; with a foreword by Nathan Glazer.
p.   cm. — (New French thought)
Includes bibliographical references and index.
ISBN 0-691-01640-2 (cloth : alk. paper)
1. Welfare state. 2. France—Economic policy. 3. France—Social policy.
I. Title. II. Series
HC276.R6513   2000
306′.0944—dc21      99-037483

Published with the assistance of the French Ministry of Culture.

This book has been composed in Adobe Bauer Bodoni

The paper used in this publication meets the minimum requirements of ANSI/NISO Z39.48-1992 (R 1997) (*Permanence of Paper*)

http://pup.princeton.edu

Printed in the United States of America

10 9 8 7 6 5 4 3 2 1

# Contents

# Foreword

BY NATHAN GLAZER

For MORE than two decades Pierre Rosanvallon has been analyzing the development and the crisis of the "welfare state," combining precise, specific knowledge with philosophical and historical depth in a way that is rare among social policy analysts. He has written several important studies on the history of political ideas in France, as well as influential books on the French welfare state. But he is fully aware of developments in the other countries of Europe and in the United States, which gives his work a unique range.

It has been common for analysts of social policy to speak of the "backwardness" of American social policy, of the "incompleteness" of American social policy, compared to the advanced welfare states of Europe. We are used in the United States to such stories as one that appeared in the *New York Times* while I was reading this book, "Child Care Sacred as France Cuts Back the Welfare State." It describes a *creche*, a municipal day care nursery, in Paris, of a lavishness in facilities and staffing that would put any public institution of the sort in the United States to shame: "To care for her 88 children, [the director] has a staff of 25 trained employees, a ratio appproaching that of a luxury hotel" (*New York Times*, December 21, 1997).

It is undoubtedly true that European countries began ensuring a degree of common protection for their working populations and providing a wide range of social services much earlier than the United States, and have gone further in guaranteeing that protection and those services. The forms of social provision have varied considerably from country to country. The role of insurance and common taxation has varied from program to program, and the degree of uniformity in benefits and protection varies from country to country. It is also true, as the story reminds us, that the welfare states of Europe are under severe financial pressure, as costs rise for pensions, health care, unemployment compensation, and a great range of social services. These problems of the welfare state are familiar, and a host of politicians and analysts ponder them every day.

Yet the crisis of the welfare state reflects larger problems than simple fiscal exigency. The large view developed in *The New Social Question,* transcends the simple notions of "backwardness" and "forwardness," of "completeness" and "incompleteness." Social developments continually surprise us: there is no finished form of the welfare state, and even the most complete efforts to ensure against all exigencies surprise us with failure. We discover we can all learn from one another. Now Europe is learning that even the England of Margaret Thatcher, with its determined withdrawal from some aspects of the welfare state, and the United States of Ronald Reagan (not so different from that of Bill Clinton) can teach lessons as well as raise alarms.

What we all face, as Rosanvallon argues, are new forms of society and economy in which common experiences in life and work, characterizing whole classes, are becoming differentiated. With this differentiation the one all-embracing program, whether for social security or unemployment insurance or health care, no longer fits all adequately, and is subject to increasing strain. This differentiation is characterized by, for example, the passing of the assembly line, in which all perform pretty much the same task under the same conditions, and its white-collar equivalent, exemplified in those old photographs of vast floors of typists or long lines of telephone operators. This differentiation is accompanied by a great increase in knowledge and our capacity to use it, such that the principle of insurance, which has been so important in so many key social programs, is threatened by a new ability to define self-interest.

"As society gains more knowledge," Rosanvallon writes, "a considerable change in the perception of fairness tends to be produced." I was reminded of a class some years ago in which a student explored the impact of the differences in life expectancy on "fairness" in social security. If blacks had shorter lives than whites, and could expect their social security benefits to cover a shorter period in retirement, should their contributions be as much as those of others'? But this is only the beginning of a differentiation of group from group, indeed individual from individual, that we can explore in this complex world of social insurance. Further analyses would lead to other results, all raising questions about the fairness for them of the one big social-insurance system. Thus, we now hear calls from the better-off, who wish to be able to withdraw from the social security system, in their belief that they can do better alone.

Thus one of the foundation stones of modern liberalism—its blindness—comes under strain. As formalized in John Rawls's influential theory of justice, liberalism has come to imply that we must derive our principles as if we lived behind a veil, ignorant of our fate. Under these conditions a principle of justice can be formulated that calls for committing ourselves to sharing equally a fate that can affect any of us. But we know so much more today about what affects the future of the individual, from the influence of genetic inheritance to the influence of family to the influence of behavior on health and stability. The veil of ignorance is torn. Consider the impact of genetic knowledge when it comes to health insurance. Should those who know from their inheritance that they are likely to escape key diseases pay for those who know their likelihood to suffer them? We try through legislation to suppress the impact of such knowledge: insurance companies shall not take this or that knowledge into account. The free market, which has been given a much larger role in post-Thatcher England and in the United States than in France or other European continental countries, can take account of such differences as easily as it takes account of niches for profit. But if the welfare state does likewise, what happens to its principles, which call on all to participate and share burdens and benefits equally?

In Rosanvallon's account, social differentiation and expanded knowledge—and the ability to act on it—are key challenges to the ideal of the welfare state. For the principle of mutual insurance was indeed established under a condition of ignorance, in which common rules and arrangements for vast numbers in a common position seemed fair and efficient. Under the new circumstances of a changing economic order, changing (or disintegrating) social rules, and expanding knowledge, only the principle of "solidarity" defends many of the traditional features of the welfare state.

This is one of those terms in Rosanvallon's discussion that will strike American ears oddly. We will have to recall that the principles of the French revolution called for "*liberté, egalité, fraternité*," and only the first two—liberty and equality—have received the wholehearted support of Americans during our two-hundred-year history. "Fraternity" or "solidarity" are not familiar terms for us, and it would be interesting to explore why. Certainly in our rhetoric and our ideals, we do want to include all Americans. When Franklin D. Roosevelt spoke of one-third of a nation ill-housed, ill-fed, ill-clothed, he was summoning up the ideals of fraternity and solidarity, without using the same words. More recent political leaders have spoken of the "family" or "village" of America.

The absence of fraternity and solidarity in American political rhetoric may remind us of a key feature of American society that finds no equivalent in France, and that has strongly shaped the development of American social policy. That key feature is the presence from the beginning of a large racial minority that was held in slavery and kept down by prejudice and discrimination, and whose economic and social condition even today, generations after the end of slavery, strikingly differentiates it from the rest of the American population.

The presence of this large excluded minority has shaped American social policy, both hampering its development and helping to force it into original paths. Here two other terms in Rosanvallon's discussion that will

strike Americans as odd must be noted: "exclusion" and "assimilation."
He is not speaking of phenomena that are strange to us, whatever the
distinctions of language. The "excluded" are those who fall outside, in one
way or another, the system of protection, either because their characteristics, capacities, and habits are such that they cannot make effective use of
the benefits of the welfare state or because the laws and rules that define
the forms of inclusion have for some reason left them out. Rosanvallon has
in mind the long-term unemployed, the homeless, and others.

We would add to them categories far more numerous here than in Europe, such as those incapacitated for normal work and family life by
drugs, and those in prison or under the authority of the system of justice.
The numbers of the excluded rise, here as in Europe. The task of society
is to "assimilate" them, and this turns out to be far more difficult than the
builders of the welfare state imagined. The welfare state always assumed
that it could count on the basic drives that so obviously determine the
social behavior of most men: they could be expected to want to earn their
daily bread, to support their wives and children, to educate and discipline
their children.

Obviously there would be exceptions and difficult cases, and there was
always social work, whether by religious and philanthropic or state-sup-
ported agencies, for difficult cases. But the difficult cases multiply under
social differentiation and social change. For some decades in the United
States we have been concerned with what we call, without great precision,
the "underclass," and have devised program after program to deal with
them: programs for work, to improve the education of their children, to
make possible more stable residences, or to cope with the consequences of
ill-health and poor habits. But the numbers have grown, here and in
France. Rosanvallon does not use the term "underclass," but his "excluded" include those we would call the underclass.

Rosanvallon surprisingly does not comment on one phenomenon that
must add to the number of the excluded and that raises special problems
concerning assimilation. This is non-European immigration, which has in
France, as in other prosperous continental countries, added a large number of foreign-born persons whose language and religion are different
from that of the native population. The foreign-born in France, Germany,
Sweden, and the Netherlands form as large a group proportionately today
as in the United States. And they and their children are far more likely to
fall among the excluded than native Europeans.

Their problems of assimilation extend beyond those that Rosanvallon
considers when he speaks of assimilation. For Rosanvallon, assimilation
means primarily gaining the experience, attitudes, and training that per-
mit stable employment, and which lead to "insertion," to use the French
term, into the society of the "included." For this purpose, France has de-

vised a program called "Revenue Minimum d'Insertion" (RMI), which is a sharp departure from traditional social policies based on insurance and benefits as of right. In Rosanvallon's description, this new program, which already encompasses one million persons, is "based on the mutual commitment of the individual and the collective to deal with the needs, aspirations, and possibilities of the beneficiaries" [83]. But there are dangers in this approach: in adapting and relating to the specific problems of the individual among the excluded, "local committees governing the RMI sometimes look like nineteenth-century charity offices, distinguishing good from bad paupers" [102].

While there are certainly differences, what Rosanvallon is describing is very similar to what local communities in the United States now face as welfare moves to "workfare." In this process, as we have discovered, no uniform rule can be laid down, which is why every state and indeed every community is left to work things out as best it can. We begin to approximate traditional social work, as exemplified, for example, in the *New York Times* Christmas appeal for the "hundred neediest cases," where each family has experienced misfortune in its own way, a way with which no uniform state policy can deal. The individual characteristics of the excluded—their "biographies," in Rosanvallon's account—must be considered, if they are to be successfully assimilated. To fit them or insert them into stable society requires differentiated means, which we are only after decades of painful experience developing.

Rosanvallon is fully aware of this long American experience. But there is even a longer French experience with this kind of problem. He uncovers for us a fascinating record of French efforts, from the time of the Revolution on, to deal with the excluded through work, and some of the problems faced from the beginning are little different from those we face today.

Whatever the changes in economy and society, some dilemmas of social policy are simply built into efforts to improve and raise individuals by common means. Consider the report of the Committee on Begging in 1790 on providing work through state workshops—making government, in contemporary terminology, the "employer of last resort":

> Take a man who—if he could not rely on work provided by the government, would seek it no matter how far away—but certain of finding it nearby, appears, says he lacks work, and he really does. Another man will avoid hard work; if he is sure of receiving easier work from the administration he will ask for it. . . . Laziness, independence, and the fortunate faculty of living from day to day will always have a great attraction for the common run of men. What means will the government have, however multiplied and however divided one may assume its means of administration, to distinguish real needs, those due to worsening circumstances, to misfortunes the worker couldn't

have anticipated or repaired himself, from the pretexts that skillfully cover laziness and lack of foresight? We would have to make a detailed study of the interests of every individual, his behavior, and all the little circumstances that can still influence the present situation. Is that conceivable? [73]

Rosanvallon does differentiate the new tasks of the welfare state from the harsh paternalism of nineteenth century charity. He insists that "the key to the initiation of a new type of welfare state is *that there are no possible obligations without corresponding jobs*" [92]. And he is aware, as his account of the Revolution's effort to deal with this principle tells us, of the problems involved. In some way, I take him to be saying, we have to combine our acknowledgment of these historic problems in social policy with our contemporary situation and our contemporary understandings.

Our social fabric is more complex than that dealt with in the past, and yet historical and traditional means of relating people to society must still play the central role in the social policy of our more complex societies: "The issue is how to recreate those forms of 'close social protection' represented primarily by the family. . . . Lacking sufficient financial resources [to do through the state what we expect the family to do], we hope to find a 'sociological' solution to the crisis of the welfare state and we dream of a coherent and stable family. The state today is not trying to promote social values (fidelity, filial piety, etc.) but social forms." We can, he hopes, avoid the "nanny state," while still restoring and upholding the connections and responsibilities that incorporate people into society. This is a difficult task, but this subtle and informed book goes a long way toward delineating what has to be done and how we can achieve it.

# The New Social Question

# The New Social Question

THE SENSE that the welfare state is in crisis has been with us since the 1970s. Yet the meaning and form of this crisis have changed considerably over recent decades. It has undergone three stages, and each of them has weakened the welfare state. The first two were financial and ideological,[1] while the last may be termed philosophical. The financial crisis was triggered in the 1970s by the slowdown in economic growth, which automatically set off a serious rise in compulsory contributions to compensate for the deficits of public finances. The 1980s was a decade of ideological crisis, fueled by the suspicion that the state could not effectively manage social problems and a dissatisfaction with an increasingly opaque and bureaucratic approach that blurred goals and led to a crisis of legitimacy.

These last two dimensions of the crisis are still with us. Control of health costs and various social benefits still constitute a fundamental preoccupation. Demographic factors (longer life-expectancy) and technical ones (medical progress) helped fuel a permanent increase in expenses, on both sides of the Atlantic. While Medicare in the United States involves only 37 million elderly or handicapped persons, it is this population whose medical costs increase most rapidly. In 1970, those costs were only $6 billion a year, while today they amount to an annual sum of $200 billion. Projections for the year 2030 indicate that Medicare might absorb 7.5 percent of the GDP, as opposed to 2.6 percent currently. The total sum of health expenses has also reached a very high level in France, currently absorbing 7 percent of the GDP. This development is cause for concern: in both countries, it has led to a silent revolution in the structure of public expenses. If medical consumption continues to advance, it is gradually going to devour available resources for other essential functions like education or research. The American case is quite striking: although health spending is only partially public, its development has had important undesired and unconsidered repercussions on other expenses. The portion of national wealth devoted to health care in the United States has grown from 4.6 percent to 13 percent since 1960, while the share devoted to education has stagnated at 3.5 percent. If the explosion of obligatory forms of contribution has finally been curbed since the mid-1980s, it is at the price of reducing certain benefits or precarious reforms, often decided in haste, on an impromptu basis.

Study of the efficiency and organization of the welfare state is essential. The reform of social policy management is on the agenda everywhere, though the acuteness of the problem varies according to national idiosyncrasies. For example, the financial regulations of a centralized government health service as in England, or of a system tightly supervised by contractual regulation as in Germany, seem more efficient than the French method, which demands universality without constraint. Administrative styles of offering assistance also vary considerably from one country to another. But these differences should not mask the most important new dimension of the crisis: a third weakening of the welfare-state, the philosophical one.

We are not yet fully aware of this philosophical crisis, nor how it is related to the new social question. This book intends to explore some of its aspects in order to help chart the new social landscape being created. Two major problems appear in the wake of the crisis: the disintegration of the traditional principles of social solidarity, and the inadequacy of "social rights" as a framework in which to resolve problems of social exclusion and fully legitimate assistance programs.

The old mechanisms that once produced social solidarity are clearly disintegrating. Solidarity used to be based on the increasing "mutualization" or sharing of social risks, so that the welfare state was conceived as a kind of *insurance society* under the "veil of ignorance," to use John Rawls's famous expression. The system, which had the advantage of producing solidarity through methods of redistribution opaque to the actors, has begun to crumble. This is particularly obvious in a country like France, where it is increasingly difficult to grasp the new social problems (like exclusion) in terms of concepts of *risk*. The development of social knowledge, and the greater visibility of the "gains" and "losses" resulting from that knowledge, has involved a lifting of the veil of ignorance. In other words, it has become much more problematic to consider the whole nation as a single class facing identical risks. At the same time, the pressure to develop more restrictive forms of sharing (that is, reduction of the size of risk-classes to coincide with the principle of actuarial neutrality) is also very strong. Other factors—including demographic developments, growing dissociation between groups of contributors and beneficiaries, increased knowledge of differences between individuals and groups—are combining to deteriorate further the insurance model of social solidarity.

The traditional conception of social rights, on the other hand, is also proving to be ineffective in dealing with major problems like exclusion. The traditional, or "compensatory," welfare state is based on the principled dissociation of economic and social factors. But in a context of mass unemployment and increasing exclusion, this vision of social rights as compensation for a temporary problem (illness, short-term unemployment, etc.) becomes inappropriate, giving rise to the pernicious effects of what I call the *passive welfare state*. Economically, it destroys solidarity by increasing the indirect costs of labor (taxes, contributions), eventually reducing employment. Socially, it then justifies the break between individual indemnification and social inclusion.

The problems posed in the United States by AFDC (Aid to Families with Dependent Children; and by the Temporary Aid for Needy Families, TANF, after 1996) and in France by the RMI (Minimum Income of Inclusion) are very similar in this respect. AFDC was the center of heated controversies in the United States during the 1970s and 1980s, which led to the establishment of TANF in 1996, marking an historic change in the welfare principles established in the 1930s. In France, the institution of a Minimum Income of Inclusion in 1988 led to a genuine revolution in the social system, establishing a guaranteed minimum income, beyond the normal system of unemployment compensation. More than one million individuals currently receive the RMI in France, about 3 percent of the adult population. Under these conditions, the links between assistance and work tend to be close. In both France and the U.S., then, marginal programs of social assistance have been transformed into ones that play a central role in social regulation. When AFDC was established in the United States, the affected population were widows or those in temporary difficulties. But by the early 1990s, more than two-thirds of those on the welfare rolls had been there for nine years or more. Similarly in France, the RMI, which was originally designed to constitute a short-term benefit of re-inclusion, has become a permanent source of revenue for a considerable population. Discussions of the nature and bases of the new social rights, and studies of the ultimately "pernicious effects" of the new assistance policies, are also similar in the two countries.

In both Europe and the United States, this is how the terms of the new social question are defined today. If the nature of assistance programs, the styles of management, and forms of collective foresight are different in the two continents, the collapse of the insurance society and the weakening of the traditional concept of social rights have led to the same challenges. In both cases, the philosophical crisis of the welfare state indicates a decisive change in the perception of society that has prevailed for more than a century. Beyond financial and management difficulties, it corresponds to a new period of modernity.

The philosophical crisis has led first to a radical reconsideration of the concept of rights as formulated by seventeenth-century liberal individualism, leading beyond the old oppositions between formal rights and real rights, social rights and political rights. Thus far, social rights have been conceived in the same terms as civil rights, a simple extension of the idea of freedom and autonomy, but this will no longer do.

Today, social rights are considered unconditional "rights." As long as the cost of these rights remained relatively small, affecting only populations in a constant state of turnover for short periods, it was possible *practically* to reason in these terms. But it is now evident that, far from being unconditional, these social rights are linked to a given state of the economy. Social rights must therefore be considered like political rights, that is, as rights that produce a certain kind of social bond and consequently are tied to certain activities. The current problems of the welfare state show the pernicious consequences of ignoring this social dimension in our individualistic societies, and the naive faith in the possibility (and by the same token, the right) of everyone living autonomously as he has chosen. For two centuries, the welfare state has constantly worked to make individuals more independent by freeing them from the obligation to rely on others. The new crisis of the welfare state, the philosophical one, forces us to end this wishful thinking and reconcile those obligations.

On the other hand, with the decline of the insurance society the very foundations of social solidarity must be redefined. Lifting the veil of ignorance has meant that the problem of social justice must now be posed in direct terms of *redistribution*. This is much more difficult because taxation and the forms of social life must also be relegitimated. This is why the issue of the *nation* becomes central today and cannot be separated from that of the welfare state. And this is also why we can no longer be satisfied with a purely procedural view of democracy. What was possible when the veil of ignorance existed is no longer possible when that veil is torn.

Clearly, discussions of law, the transformations of democracy, and the modes of financing social expenses are closely connected. It would be an illusion to believe that the financial aspects of the welfare state can be considered autonomously. In this respect, liberals and conservatives in both countries will be forced to reformulate the very terms of their philosophies of the civic and social bond. Wherever we look today, we see that the issue of the welfare state has become inseparable from that of work. In the United States, as in France, the problem is not simply knowing how to finance increasing social expenses in a period of budgetary restriction but, rather, the economic re-inclusion of populations who have been excluded from the world of work. In the United States, the issue of *non-work* is directly linked to the situation of the African-American population, while it presents diffuse and more complex aspects in France. But the current disjunction between political citizenship and social inclusion is spurring identical studies of the problem in both countries.

Although *The New Social Question* places the transformations of the welfare state in France in a broad philosophical perspective, it is not confined strictly to the French situation. It is intended to contribute more broadly to an analysis and resolution of problems that are becoming increasingly common to all modern societies.

# PART ONE

# Reorganizing Solidarity

# The Decline of the Insuring Society

THE WELFARE STATE developed historically through the establishment of compulsory insurance covering the major risks of life (illness, unemployment, retirement, disability, etc.). To appreciate the extent of the crisis threatening this system today, we must first recall the considerable practical and philosophical importance of collective insurance for the construction of modern society and for the establishment of the institutions that guarantee social solidarity.

### The Forms of Solidarity

The intellectual history of insurance fits into the modern investigation of the forms of social solidarity. In traditional societies, the principle of social cohesion was part of the very structure of society. Hierarchies and distinctions, as well as equivalences, bound men together organically. The social bond was perceived as *natural*, since it concerned the family, neighborhood connections, or the social hierarchy as a whole. Attempting to liberate itself from traditional systems and their emphasis on the natural links between humans, modern society thinks of itself in completely different terms and must define new types of social relations. Ever since the seventeenth century, theoreticians of natural law have elaborated contractual doctrines of society, which assume that the social bond is the result of a voluntary and artificial foundation. In this perspective, the invisible hand of the market is perceived as a kind of natural force, and accordingly as a rival to the contractual establishment of the social bond. These notions have all been analyzed and developed well enough so that we need not dwell on them. But what has not been sufficiently emphasized is the role of the idea of insurance in that search for instruments and institutions designed to free man from the chains of nature. "Foresight is the second salvation of the human race," said Mirabeau, significantly extending the formula applied by Adam Smith to the benefits of the division of labor.

At the end of the seventeenth century, Leibniz defended insurance as an instrument of justice. While Hobbes saw the state as the main "reducer of uncertainty," Leibniz considered compulsory mutual insurance to be the right solution to the problem of risk.[1] In this perspective, insurance became a substitute for the social contract by producing the same effects of group protection. Although various insuring techniques had appeared much earlier, they had been used only for wealth and merchandise, particularly in shipping. Not until the eighteenth century were they considered applicable to persons. At that time, there were three available models for conceiving of the social bond: the contract (resulting from a conscious political decision), the market (operating as an invisible hand linking men economically), and insurance (acting as a kind of invisible hand of solidarity).

In 1788, Clavière, a close colleague of Brissot and Condorcet, presented a well-developed *Prospectus de l'établissment des assurances sur la vie* (Prospectus for the Establishment of Life Insurance), a genuine programmatic manifesto of the insurance society. "Life insurance," he explained in this text, "comes to the aid of the precious sentiment that attaches an individual to other individuals who are to survive him. It prepares a guarantee against misfortune without harming either industry or activity."[2] He claimed that insurance brings men together, instituting a virtual social contract. Hence his conception of an establishment "authorized, protected, and supervised by the government." Clavière followed this vision to the end, maintaining that insurance allows the issue of poverty to be addressed in a radically new light: it prevents the sequence of misfortunes by controlling the precariousness that causes them. As he noted of his company: "The success of its establishment is necessarily linked to the decrease of begging. It is mainly from this point of view that it becomes interesting for all persons who see this calamity as the saddest malady of civilization. Plans for curing it abound; but none has yet presented a satisfying solution. The resources furnished by the doctrine of life insurance are presented so far as the surest means of reducing this scourge and preventing it in the future."[3]

At the same time, another pioneer, Piarron de Chamousset, published the *Plan d'une maison d'association* (Plan for a Joint Company), based on a system of health insurance whose subscribers would have all appropriate aid in case of illness.[4] The notion that contributions alone created obligations was new for the age: the mechanism that is instituted is not within the scope of any of the traditional mechanisms of solidarity (aid being bound, for example, to a condition of corporate affiliation).

These innovative views, formulated in the final days of the ancien régime, remained marginal, however. As applied to persons and no longer to wealth, the principle of insurance still stirred fears that it would undermine the sense of responsibility and lead to immoral behavior and pernicious calculations. Such reluctance lasted almost a century. For quite some time the virtue of foresight, which gives individuals a sense of responsibility by making them think of their future, was contrasted with insurance, which was suspected of promoting carelessness. It was not until the end of the nineteenth century that insurance was recognized as an adequate and morally acceptable response to the management of social problems.

There are several reasons for this change. First, the appeal to the sense of individual responsibility was obviously not enough to eliminate the spectre of poverty. Hence, the ideal of foresight, on which the first half of the nineteenth century had relied to overcome the hazards of life, no longer seemed sufficient. The contrast between insurance and foresight did endure for quite a while, as can be seen in the early-twentieth-century debate about compulsory retirement, the last line of resistance of classical liberalism. An economist like Paul Leroy-Beaulieu thus rebelled against the plan of compulsory retirement insurance, noting in *L'Économiste français* (The French Economist): "It weakens human responsibility and dissuades people from occupations involving initiative and independence. It is part of that whole system of social automatism which it claims to substitute for individual responsibility."[5] But that was a rearguard struggle.

### The Insuring Society

The introduction of insurance into the management of society succeeded gradually because it allowed a way out of the dilemmas of a purely individualistic view of society. Ever since the French Revolution, the major problem had been reconciling the *principle of solidarity* (society has a debt toward its members) with the *principle of responsibility* (each individual is master of his own life and must take control of himself), and linking rights with behavior, as it were. The solution was not self-evident. In fact, the limitation of the right to public aid initially presupposed that the sphere of application of individual responsibility could be clearly identified in social life. What happened was quite the opposite: industrial economic development progressively demonstrated the limits of a system of social regulation solely governed by the principles of individual responsibility and contract. In the area of responsiblity, it became increasingly difficult to discern what could be imputed to the individual and what depended on other factors. This was shown clearly by François Ewald in an analysis of work accidents: in nineteenth-century France, the increasing complexity of the processes of production made juridical categories established by Napoleon's Civil Code of 1804 inadequate.[6] In several cases, it was impossible to identify a localized infraction involving the direct responsibility of an individual in order to determine who had to compensate for the damage. Hence, when the hundredth annivesary of the Civil Code was celebrated in 1904, jurists made a long list of all areas and objects that could no longer be adequately handled within its framework.

In terms of pure economics, the persistence of poverty produced the same disruptions in the classical liberal vision. The French revolutionaries of 1789 had regarded the right to assistance as a *limited right*, and doubly so: for them, assistance was at the very limit of the rights that could be guaranteed by a general, automatic rule, and it had a limited scope, a supplemental and provisional character. From their point of view, the progress of civilization, based on the development of the division of labor and the extension of property, was to confirm this character; moreover, they were not far from considering idleness as a vice encouraged by despotism, hence also destined to a decline.

In nineteenth-century France, on the other hand, the sphere of application of this "limited" right expanded gradually. First, it became increasingly difficult to distinguish between the individual victim of misfortune (the worthy poor) and the improvident or calculating idler, the criterion of responsibility often becoming slippery. Second, the problems of assistance, which were assumed to be well circumscribed, in fact tended to dissolve into the larger framework of overall state policy. This factor, linked to the increase of poverty, is probably the most important one. While, during the French Revolution, Constituents and Conventionals had considered the issue of assistance as a philosophically central but economically marginal problem, by 1830 French politicians had to confront an expansion of poverty that was identified with the progress of industrialization itself. The difference between industrial poverty and the old notion of indigence led to a complete change of perspective. Indeed, it amounted to posing the question of property and the right to work in unprecedented terms.

As far as public aid is concerned, the legislation adopted during the French Revolution assumed that there were only two categories of relevant adults: the disabled who could not work and the able-bodied who did not find work. This legislation did not imagine for a moment that a working man could have such a low income-level that he could almost be considered a pauper. Yet it is this phenomenon, on a large scale, that developed in the nineteenth century. While the eighteenth-century pauper was an individual, nineteenth-century poverty was a massive social fact, prevailing within the working class: it represents the advent of a new type of collective social condition, the proletariat. This social condition could not be treated with simple aid: it called into question the very foundations of social organization, threatening to break down the old cohesion between property rights and the right to assistance. Hence the perplexity of the nineteenth-century classical liberals, a "class" perplexity, perhaps, but also a philosophical perplexity.

The application of insurance to social problems allowed a way out of these difficulties. Going from the subjective notion of behavior and individual responsibility to the objective notion of risk, insurance changed our perspective on society. It allowed going beyond the earlier dilemmas on the application of social rights. Indeed, by approaching social problems in terms of risk, insurance focuses on the probabilistic and statistical dimension of society (risk can be calculated) and relegates judgment about individuals to a secondary level. When situations are perceived in terms of risk, the question of personal mistakes and individual attitudes becomes less important, as was quite evident in the 1898 French law on compensation for work accidents. Furthermore, the approach in terms of risk has the advantage of bringing together a number of different problems: illness, old age, unemployment, and various kinds of accidents are gathered into a single category. Finally, it allows a new understanding of the practice of justice. It replaces the classic idea of justice, understood as conformity to nature or to an ethical or political norm, with the idea of a purely contractual justice (the system of compensation). Unlike assistance, social insurance is not simply a granted aid, it represents the execution of a contract involving the state and its citizens. Benefits are an obligation, not an act of generosity. Hence the enthusiasm shown by lawyers for the insuring principle in the second half of the nineteenth century.

By 1865, Émile Laurent, the great French theoretician of "mutualism" (insurance schemes within a single professional or union group), waxed lyrical on the subject:

> Unemployment itself, and the progress of industry, abandoned or ruined industries, in short, poverty fought in all its aspects, who knows where the genius of association and insurance might not reach someday. Insurance! We have placed it quite high, at the rank it deserves in the hierarchy of social remedies. . . . Fires and bad weather, disease and hailstorms, shipwrecks and flooding, all the scourges of the physical world can be cushioned by insurance; and industrial crises, too, and the human being himself considered as a genuine productive capital by the use of his faculties and destined to disappear someday by a disastrous event independent of his will: death. Insurance can penetrate everywhere; based on the law of large numbers, it can make savings yield a profit everywhere, so that the chances of success are much greater than the chances of failure and loss, it can introduce order into disorder, it can abolish risk, and regulate uncertainty, if not do away with it altogether.[7]

The reduction of uncertainty, which was formerly considered from the viewpoint of the protector state, could now be carried out almost technically by insuring mechanisms.

A new path was henceforth opened to social policies, a path that did not need juridical or moral justifications. For this reason, classical liberals finally understood that the establishment of a system of social insurance would allow them to avert the spectre of socialism.[8] As for the socialists, they saw this establishment as the first stage of the realization of that same socialism, as Benoît Malon clearly expressed in his programmatic work *Le Socialism intégral* (Integral Socialism), advocating the creation of a Ministry of Social Insurance.[9]

As soon as it is universalized by becoming compulsory, insurance acquires a genuinely social dimension, and plays the role of a *moral and social transformer*. Social insurance functions like an invisible hand, producing security and solidarity without the intervention of good will. Structurally, insurance concerns a vast population: by making each one part of a whole, it thus makes individuals interdependent. François Ewald sums it up clearly: "Insurance allows everyone to benefit from the advantages of the whole, while leaving him free to live as an individual. It seems to reconcile the two antagonistic terms: society and individual freedom."[10] If so, insurance is certainly an institution of the social contract, which is why the state and insurance technology converge from the middle of the nineteenth century on: they embody two complementary figures of the reduction of uncertainty. In the 1850s, Émile de Girardin defined the state significantly as a "universal insurer":[11] for this reason, in his terms, it becomes the "earthly paradise."[12] Such a notion was still far from the fact at that time and had to wait to be implemented until the establishment of Social Security in France in 1945. But at least it was clearly formulated at that period.

## The Crisis of a Model

It is this *insurance paradigm*, the inseparably technical and philosphical basis of the welfare state, which is currently wearing out. The power of the original idea of Social Security, as formulated and implemented in France, stemmed from the synthesis it had achieved: it allowed a very broad spectrum of social problems to be considered coherently by reducing them to the homogeneous category of risk. Illness, unemployment, even old age were understood as risks when they were perceived in terms of loss of income.

By now, however, the unifying category of risk has lost a great deal of its relevance. Simple distinctions between the sick or disabled and the healthy, employed and unemployed, working and retired, assume that all individuals run the same kind of risks. The implicit principle of justice and solidarity that underlies the welfare state is based on the idea that risks were both equally distributed and largely unpredictable. Clearly this is not the case today, when social problems can no longer be perceived solely in terms of risk. Phenomena of exclusion, such as long-term unemployment, unfortunately often define *stable conditions*. Thus we move from an unpredictable and circumstantial approach of "social breakdowns" to a more deterministic view, in which situations of breakdown cannot easily be reversed. Because of that, a whole section of the population is no longer part of the world of insurance. This has been clear for a long time for retirement, which could not be dealt with strictly with insurance logic per se, unless the case was seen in terms of disability insurance.[13]

This transformation has had an incredibly broad scope. Dependence, for example, is a problem concerning an increasing number of elderly persons: France currently numbers 1.5 million dependent elderly persons, and the National Institute of Statistical and Economic Information (INSEE) predicts that by the year 2000, six hundred thousand elderly persons will be severely dependent, requiring daily aid; eight hundred thousand elderly persons will be semi-dependent, needing aid several times a week; and five hundred thousand elderly persons will be occasionally dependent.  Can that be conceived as a risk? Probably not. Neither a handicap nor an illness, dependence—except when it can be equated with a disability resulting from an accident in young people—is an unpredictable phenomenon.[14] If dependence must be taken care of, it can only be done in the mode of an overall national solidarity.[15] Insurance thus appears ill-equipped to deal with a problem of that nature. As far as society is concerned, the central concept today is much more that of precariousness or vulnerability than that of risk.[16] Accordingly, the old instruments of social management become obsolete.

The notion of risk is certainly still relevant. But it has changed its scale, as has been correctly emphasized.[17] An increasingly serious problem today is *catastrophic risk*: natural risks (floods, earthquakes), major technological accidents, large-scale damage to the environment. These threats no longer concern individuals, but entire populations, even nations. The distribution of the risks undertaken by insurance can no longer be operative in this case, as was realized clearly when the issue involved finding an adequate framework to compensate victims of natural catastrophes. For some time, this was handled as assistance: the state could distribute emergency aid (an Aid Fund for victims of disasters and calamities was created for this purpose in France in 1956), but without formulating any legal framework the victims could have referred to. In this case, the allocation of compensation was within the scope of generosity and not law. The law of July 1982 on compensation for natural disasters changed that situation. But to do so, it had to combine the notions of solidarity and of insurance in a hybrid fashion. The system established by the law remains an insuring one, since it is based on the individual payment of premiums on current

insurance, but it is also akin to a logic of solidarity: the implementation of
the system is consistently tied to a public procedure (leading to the decree
of a natural catastrophe) and the premiums paid are uniform, as are the
risks (if, for example, the insurance principle applies among the inhabitants of flood zones, the premiums of persons living in non-flood zones are
pure contributions of solidarity).

The principles underlying Social Security cease to operate in such cases
of major collective risks. Moreover, in a technologically developed society,
the risk of catastrophe becomes increasingly important,[18] and under-
standably, new procedures of mutualization are devised to meet it. By
changing the scale, major risk produces a new approach to the social
bond: it leads, in fact, to radicalizing the vision of society as a community
of fate. Confronted with the threat of a nuclear accident, for example, all
barriers and distinctions between men are wiped out, the solidarity reflex
becomes evident without any discussion.

In addition, our societies also recover a more distinct sense of individual
responsibility. To a large extent, the development of the insuring society
had led to the socialization of responsibility, and the assignment of blame
had become less important than the search for a satisfactory system of
compensation. The great French jurist Saleilles wrote in this vein: "Modern life, more than ever, is an issue of risk. . . . The issue is not to inflict a
penalty but to know who must bear the damages, the one who caused it or
the one who experienced it. The penal point of view is out of the question,
only the social point of view is involved. It is no longer an issue of responsibility, strictly speaking, but an issue of risks."[19] This was the direction of
the pioneering law of 1898 on work accidents, an approach that remains
valid in many respects. For example, the idea of treating medical malpractice in this perspective is making headway.[20]

But a movement in the other direction, in what might be called the
American way, is also emerging in France: on all sides, "irresponsible"
society is denounced, and individuals are called upon to take responsibility for themselves. A similar return to individual responsibility is also emphasized in politics, although for different reasons. Furthermore, the traditional system of compensation for accidents is proving to be inadequate
to deal with collective accidents like HIV-contamination of blood transfu-
sions. As long as accidents are individual, the system of the socialization of
responsibility established by the French law of 1898 for work accidents, or
the law of 1985 for pedestrian accidents, does function satisfactorily. But
accidents concerning entire *populations* demand different mechanisms for
assuming responsibility which can be public only up to a certain point.

Thus, the French law of December 31, 1991, created a special fund to compensate hemophiliacs and patients who received blood contaminated with
the AIDS virus.[21]

For this twofold reason, the classical way of putting the notion of social risk at the base of the welfare state tends to lose its relevance. This notion disintegrates from top to bottom: attention to catastrophic risk on the one hand, and return to the individual error on the other, combine to reduce its importance. Of course, there are areas in which the procedure of the socialization of responsibility by insurance still seems applicable. Several recent drafts of French laws, for example, have suggested considering medical risk, whatever the origin and seriousness of the consequences incurred, as a social risk, assumed by a procedure analogous to that of work accidents. But that is an isolated case.

Another factor must still be taken into account to assess fully the social implications of the transformations that affect our conception of the notion of risk: this factor is the parallel evolution of our perception of *insecurity*. During the "Thirty Glorious Years" of French economic development (1948–78), the risk of loss of income constituted the main social danger, but this is no longer the case, even if economic insecurity, linked to the employment situation, is still significant. New forms of social insecurity appear—urban crime, family disintegration, international dangers, etc.—which sometimes relate back to the classical state more than to the welfare state: social protection again exends to physical security, producing a different relationship of individuals to the state. Social Security no longer appears as the binding center of social progess; from now on, it covers only a part of society.

### The Inborn and the Acquired

Another factor is also going to contribute to a profound undermining of the social security system: the progress of medical genetics, which will produce a considerable revolution in our perception of the relation of individuals to society and in our spontaneous approach to solidarity, a revolution whose direction and scope we are only just beginning to see. In brief, the progress of genetics is moving toward a radical reevaluation of the analysis of health risks, leading to a view of the social that is both more individualistic and more deterministic.

The distinctive feature of genetic knowledge, as it appears in the large research project of the human genome, is to change our concept of disease.[22] Where we once saw only hazard and bad luck, genetic medicine now detects *predictable* organic causes. Initially, they discovered that some pathologies were distinguished by genes whose possession automatically led the individual concerned to develop a given type of disease. So far, three thousand so-called monogenic ailments have been identified. An examination of an embryo can now tell if an individual will develop certain diseases. On the other hand, scientists are also able to be increasingly precise in evaluating the genetic predispositions of each individual to develop several other diseases.

The notion of risk changes its meaning in this framework. It can no longer be understood in an overall statistical model, as, for example, when we calculate that each individual has one chance in $x$ of dying of liver cancer. With genetic knowledge, we go from the group to the individual in order to personalize the risk. Of course, accidents or diseases whose development is completely unpredictable do still exist, and in many cases, the knowledge of innate risk should be adjusted by factoring in behavior, as with cardiovascular conditons, for example. If we now know more about the nature of strictly genetic tendencies that can produce arteriosclerosis and thrombosis, we also know that external variables of behavior (smoking, exercise) intervene. Hence, we must not leap to the conclusion that the health of every individual is inevitably programmed. Indeed, in most cases, "predictive medicine" continues to formulate diagnoses in terms of probabilities. Statistical reasoning is still essential.

Nevertheless, this predictive medicine has introduced a break that profoundly changes our perception of relations between the inborn and the acquired. We now strive toward the establishment of individual actuarial tables resulting from the compound of the acquired and the inborn.[23] Risk still exists, but it is no longer pure chance (that is, an unpredictable event); it becomes more individualized. Now, we go from the group to the individual to comprehend risk. As summed up by Professor Jean Bernard: "The medicine of the future will be individualized. We have been told often enough that the medicine of the future would be a medicine of herds, a collective, gregarious medicine. What is produced is completely the opposite. Medicine concerns man, one man, this unique man who is different from all the others."[24]

These developments in genetics will eventually have enormous social and political consequences simply because they will replace the statistical approach to the social with models that will take account of *personal* determinisms and behaviors. By the same token, the insuring logic underlying the welfare state is invalidated, since insurance consists of subordinating individual data to the statistically general charactistics of a population. Insurance functions essentially for socialization, aggregation, solidification. The risks covered by the insurer affect vast populations, and insurance can exist only if such populations are homogeneously constituted so that the risks run by the individuals who compose them can be mutualized. Given this notion of risk, insurance can develop an artificial and contractual legal framework in which equity is no longer perceived as conformity to nature. But if the inborn prevails over the acquired, this conception of justice collapses. In fact, the very notion of insurable risk disappears if risks are personalized: insurance is impossible when determinations are individual, for in this case, strictly speaking, there is no longer any unpredictablity. There would be nothing to mutualize if men were completely fixed in their nature.

We have not reached that point yet, and we need not worry that genetics will chain man to his fate by denying his freedom. But predictive medicine does destroy one of the mainsprings of our societies: the belief in the progressive emancipation from natural forces as an implicit law of human progress. The veil of ignorance (as John Rawls called it) that accompanied the social contract is now irreparably torn. From now on, we shall have to rethink solidarity, with clearer knowledge of the situation and chances of each individual. The accepted norms of justice will have to be defined in the direct encounter between groups and individuals. The exercise of solidarity will become more directly political; it will be identified with the formulation of the social contract itself. Today, this revolution in the knowledge of individual fate only affects private insurance, where the classes of risk are refined and differentiated according to existing knowledge, thus leading to an increasing segmentation of the social.

Today, a new force of disintegration is invisibly at work in the progress of information and will inevitably affect the universe of social insurance. The acceptance of solidarity is now beginning to be accompanied by a demand for control over personal behavior. The smoker will soon be required to choose between his vice and the right to equal access to care, and the alcoholic will be threatened with payment of social surcharges. As the social cost of individual attitudes appears more distinctly, solidarity and freedom will part company. The decline of the insuring society is also manifested in this way.

### Hidden Redistributions

The preceding arguments point to the decline of the insuring society. An examination of the institutional breakup of the system suggests that we are moving progressively toward the "logic of solidarity," by which I mean a system of direct redistribution, rather than a general insurance scheme under the veil of ignorance. For a long time, social insurance experienced an intense process of growth. In Europe in 1910, only 15 percent of the population was actively benefitting from a system of public social insurance, while the rate of coverage is certainly almost complete by now, even if the French system has in fact failed to establish a truly universal system of social security. Corporate and socioprofessional particularisms, as well as an old suspicion toward mutual insurance, left a segmented system in place.[25]

Every insuring system is redistributive, its redistribution being purely compensatory: it is intended to offset damages and proceeds as a horizontal redistribution. However, mechanisms of vertical redistribution between economic classes which are essentially solidarist have, however, gradually developed within the social security system. But since this movement has been carried out piecemeal, we may not always be aware of its extent. Without getting into technical details, we can briefly indicate the broad features of the development toward a system that is vertically more redistributive.

First, the ceiling on several social contributions (health insurance, in particular) has gradually been lifted, while the benefits paid are independent of income, and are the same for everyone. While the system established in France in 1945 limited contributions to a certain level (called a ceiling), on the principle that medical consumption was not a function of salary, financing needs have led to a lifting of the ceiling. Thus, from 1967 to 1984, in a series of small adjustments, the nature of medical insurance changed. Quite unobtrusively, whenever the ceiling has been lifted, the premium increases have been perceived as a purely "short-term" contribution to balance the accounts of Social Security. The 1983 White Paper on social protection, for example, noted that lifting the ceiling "might constitute both a means of releasing new resources and a first step toward a more equitable distribution of the social effort." The same process has also affected other contributions such as those concerning work accidents (law of January 23, 1990) or family subsidies (law of 1990).[26]

From the 1980s on, a set of other measures has continued the redistributive effects of these liftings of the ceiling. As of 1982, state employees in France have had to pay a contribution of 1 percent to finance unemployment insurance, even though they themselves enjoy employment tenure and are not at such risk. This is a contribution whose official designation—"A special contribution of solidarity with workers deprived of employment"—is sufficient to indicate its nature. The origin of unemployment insurance is particularly significant here. Established in 1958, the system of the UNEDIC (National Union for Employment in Trade and Industry), is a joint-controlled organization managing the unemployment benefit payments. This system arose from the idea of an individual insurance taken by workers against the risk of being temporarily out of work. The original mission of the UNEDIC was gradually expanded to a genuine generalized welfare for people without work, whether they are unemployed in the strict sense of the term or not.

In 1994, French unions and employers signed a national agreement openly anticipating that retirees would be called upon to guarantee the rescue of the retirement system for executives (AGIRC), thus contradicting the system's founding principle. Moreover, in 1974 a law instituted procedures of demographic compensation between wage-earners and non-wage-earners. This measure generated considerable anxiety in the 1970s about the famous "unwarranted burdens" on the Social Security funds (health insurance in particular); that is, expenses that were different from social insurance, strictly speaking: compensation between social systems, payment by Social Security of expenses pertaining to national solidarity (payment of the contributions of handicapped adults, for example), payment of benefits to noncontributing populations, etc.[27]

In France, the various social security departments (health, old age, family, work accidents) are theoretically independent, using individual instruments of management and separate accounts. But that division increasingly tends to represent only a façade. French Social Security now forms a vast, polymorphous system, with vague boundaries and complex financing, in which contributions, loans, subsidies, and all sorts of transfers have become inextricably mingled. Although the strict separation of risks and systems is still loudly asserted by officials, the reality is quite different. Moreover, this development has been accelerated since the 1980s by the rise in unemployment, the erosion of the salary base, and the resultant decrease in the number of those who contribute. Public policies of exemptions or reduction of social burdens to encourage businesses to create jobs have only increased this process. While the number of employees exempted from paying the premiums was only 181,000 in 1984, it reached over 1,000,000 in 1992. Since their private contributions are only partially recompensed by the state, they lead in fact to a new form of income redistribution. Considering that health insurance benefits were progressively expanded, from 1967 to 1978, to categories of noncontributors, we can assess the vast discrepancy between the theoretical principles that form the base of the institutions of social security and the reality of their functioning. Thus, social insurance was profoundly transformed during the 1970s and 1980s, producing a new relationship between insurance and solidarity that was never formulated by the founding fathers of the system, so that we can now talk of the "myth of insurance."[28]

This is even true now of the least mobile area, that of retirement. A study by the National Fund of Old Age Insurance in the 1980s assessed the rate of the noncontributive share of the bulk of pensions at 30 percent.[29] As for the old divisions of retirement based on professions, they have been completely dismantled by demographic development and cannot even meet their obligations. Some spectacular figures can be cited.[30] In 1950, the proportion of agricultural workers numbered 1,228 million contributors to 161,000 retirees, that is, a ratio of 8:1; in 1987, there were 682,000 contributors to 1,521 million retirees, the demographic ratio thus falling to 2:5. The case of the section of mines is even more extraordinary: in 1950, 405,000 dues-payers had to support 243,000 pensioners (a ratio of 1.67:1), which was difficult even then; but the situation became completely impossible in 1987 when there were only 60,000 workingmen to 437,000 retirees (a ratio of 0.14:1)! Here, too, the system works only with moves of hidden redistribution. Under these conditions, the old mutual-benefit logic, based on professional divisions, disappears. In an increasingly complex and advanced world, solidarity can only be global.

### The Effects of the Demographic Revolution

Demographic data have also contributed to changing our perception of equity. Behind social protection from risks, it has become increasingly apparent that the welfare state has also functioned as an enormous machine for transfers between generations. If one of the goals of the welfare state is to guarantee a function of "deferment," that is, the provision of its benefits over a life cycle, the conditions of exercising that function have led to profound imbalances between generations.[31] In two decades, the original logic of the welfare state has silently weakened under the consequences of the demographic revolution (increased life expectancy on the one hand, and a decrease in the birth rate on the other), progressively yielding to a new society of transfers.[32]

This is true, first, of health insurance, as emphasized by several studies: health expenses are now concentrated in the upper age brackets. Medical consumption in France from the ages of twenty to sixty (the age of the contributors) averages three times less than that of those between eighty and ninety years old.[33] Clearly, contributions to health insurance do not serve primarily to cover the expenses of the insured contributors: they mainly benefit retirees (only some of whom can contribute and at a relatively symbolic rate).[34]

These intergenerational transfers do not stop there, but can also be observed in incomes (because of the importance in France of seniority in remuneration) or inheritance. But it is naturally in the area of retirement pensions that they are most obvious. In an essay eloquently titled *Génération sacrifiée: les 20–45 ans* (Sacrificed Generation: 20–45-Year-Olds), Christian Saint-Étienne presents a harsh but correct diagnosis: "For ten years, those between 30 and 45 years old have borne the highest rate of compulsory deductions in our history and the heaviest of all the large industrial countries . . . while, in the period 1980–2000, those over 60 benefit from the highest average level of pensions in history, along with an unprecedented level of care assumed by society, and considerable income from a patrimony concentrated mainly in their hands." And further: "In the 80s and the first half of the 90s, the young have experienced a very high rate of unemployment. . . . And when they reach retirement age, they will be subjected to the greatest conceivable collective lowering of purchasing power."[35]

The White Paper on retirement pensions, published in the spring of 1991, did not hesitate to brandish the spectre of a war between generations, when mentioning these economic data. In his preface to that work, Michel Rocard was right to call it "a new contract between the generations." We need to rethink the very forms of equity today, as perceptions of equity gradually become more complex. Thus, the deceptively simple idea of "reduction of inequalities" (generally understood as an instant reduction of income disparity) has gradually been joined by the notions of *intergenerational equity* or the *new equity of opportunities* (aiming at equity in situations over time and not only at equity of starting point).

## *The Decline of Joint Control*

Despite its progressive disintegration, this system has long maintained an appearance of cohesion because of the organizational identity conferred on it in France by the principle of joint control of employers and labor unions. Joint control is very important in maintaining the fiction of an insurance society. In the ideology and practice of the labor unions, their participation in the management of Social Security was prized as a symbol that the system belonged to the workers (an objective, moreover, that was strongly advanced in 1945 by the founding fathers of Social Security in France). The elections of salaried administrators of the Social Security divisions—which are currently postponed *sine die*—also played a significant part in the social legitimation of the role of the unions. But the crisis of social representation and the weakening of unionism, along with the increasing intervention of the state to plug up the holes of the various divisions, have undermined the edifice.[36] The law of spring 1994 on social protection symbolically supported this development requiring an annual parliamentary discussion of the finances of Social Security. Taking place at the final stages of the adoption of the budget, this discussion is supposed to lead to a vote on a "projected target" of the expenses of Social Security. Even if this vote is not meant to have any constraining legal effects, the new procedure does dramatically indicate the decline of joint control.

All these factors have contributed to the decline of the welfare state in its traditional form. Did this process simply translate the obliteration of the "Bismarckian" model, based on the mechanism of social insurance in which benefits are the counterpart of contributions, into the "Beveridgian" model, which supplies uniform benefits to all citizens and is financed by taxation, its benefits often constituting only rather low minimums.[37]

Nothing is less certain. For althought the Bismarckian welfare state is indeed eroding, it is not the system imagined by Beveridge that is winning. Everything is pushing the new welfare state currently under construction toward more solidarity, but the original Beveridgian mechanism is not the solution for the future. Adapted to the postwar historical context, it has certainly established a universalist system based on citizenship, but it provides only extremely minimal benefits. To make the system viable, Great Britain has had to establish a whole combination of complementary, nonuniversalist aid allowances. Thus the Beveridgian model must also be amended, for it has not weathered the crisis of the welfare state any better than the Bismarckian model. Beyond the historical difference between the two models, it is the principle of solidarity itself that must be rethought.

## CHAPTER 2

# Remaking a Nation

THE ISSUE of the welfare state is becoming increasingly synonymous with the issue of citizenship. As the insurance foundations of the system are eroded, a logic of solidarity must take over, reducing everything to the essential, where social and civic bonds merge. Citizenship is inseparable from a sort of moral covenant. Communal life rests on a simple arithmetic: the obligations of the collective toward each of its members are equal to the involvement of those members. Because citizens are willing to die for the homeland, the homeland is indebted to them. War institutes a principle of radical equivalence, where each life has the same weight. The welfare state is a peacetime and mundane version of that ideal, based on the same impulse.

Thus, there are two possible ways of telling the history of the welfare state: as an institutional history, by analyzing the application and extension of insurance techniques to society; or as a philosophical history, concerning the notion of citizenship, relating social rights with the state's obligation toward individuals, thus embedding the history of the welfare state in that of the nation-state. For some time, the first type of history has prevailed, demonstrating the technical construction of the edifice of French Social Security, and providing a better understanding of the legal and practical conditions of the progression from traditional assistance to the modern welfare state. But the current context demands a return to a more philosophical and political approach. The earthquake of mass unemployment in France forces us to confront the essential nature of the welfare state rooted in the social contract itself.

## Social Citizenship

The establishment of the current institutions in France was part of a trend toward universalizing mutual insurance in society. But the establishment of the French system of 1946 had to overcome hidden social resistance, especially among employers, as well as heavy political burdens. In this respect, the modern history of French Social Security must be considered

in tandem with the reinforcement of the civic bond produced by the two
world wars. In 1930, one of the supporters of the first French law of social
insurance expressed this notion cogently, emphasizing that the law "was
born, right after the war, from the solidarity established between the various social classes; from the will to grant help necessary in bad times to
those who had defended the homeland in the trenches; from the memory
of their efforts; from a great idea of national solidarity."[1] This analysis
goes to the heart of the issue, demonstrating why the welfare state in
France has progressed by leaps and bounds, especially during crises that
produce a more or less explicit reformulation of the social contract. The
experience of war is particularly illustrative, since it radicalizes the course
of lives and reduces the social bond to its basic origin. The founder of the
English system of social security, Beveridge, correctly insisted on its equal-
izing effect. "The most general effect of war," he explained, is that "every
able-bodied person in the community becomes an asset."[2] Threatening to
return men to a state of nature, war thus provokes an experience of social
cohesion, as noted in March 1944 in one of the major journals of the French
Resistance, *Cahiers de défense de la France* (Journal of the Defense of
France): "The moment is propitious for reaffirming the social unity of the
nation."[3]

The bond between the implementation of the welfare state and the reformulation of the social contract was very strong in France after World
War II, as indicated in the preamble to the law of October 4, 1945, concerning the organization of Social Security. To justify the institution of a
system of social security, this document referred to the "spirit of brotherhood and reconciliation of classes that marks the end of the war." The
French minister of labor and social security at that time, Ambroise
Croizat, also noted that the reform was "born of the terrible ordeal we
have just experienced."[4]

The notion of rooting social rights in an arithmetic of social debt existed
long before the twentieth century. For example, the major systems of compensation or the most organized systems of social welfare established during the French Revolution were broadly linked to the management of the
social consequences of the war. The Revolutionary leaders intended to
follow Rousseau's exhortation to "let their country therefore be a common
mother to all the citizens."[5] They issued repeated solemn assurances that
aid to the poor was a "sacred debt," and declared a monthly holiday to
honor misfortune.[6] Clearly, the welfare state owes more to Rousseau than
to Marx. But beyond this general notion is the strictly *patriotic* dimension
of assistance, which was truly central at that time. By 1791, a whole series
of decrees granted aid on a patriotic basis: aid to the Acadian and Canadian refugees in France, and later to several other categories of refugees;
compensation for property damage suffered during the enemy invasion;

aid to parents of victims of August 10, 1792, of the day of the Champ-de-Mars, etc. In autumn 1792, aid for families of the homeland's defenders constituted one of the central themes of public assistance policy in France.[7] A planned *Code des secours publics* (Code of Public Aid), developed in the Year II, stated: "The nation owes a great deal to the citizens who volunteered to defend freedom, and so it has granted them several advantages; to demonstrate its respect and gratitude, it has decided to include their families in the effects of its generosity. If the fortune of battle turns against them, aid of all kind is still offered them and their families. The provisions of this part of the code are the most extensive."[8] Throughout the period of the Directory, those forms of patriotic aid remained very active, and came to form a vast operation just before 18 Brumaire.

The civic dimension of the welfare state is not unique either to France or to England, but was also a decisive factor in the United States, as demonstrated by Theda Skocpol. Her illuminating study highlighted the critical role in the construction of a "maternal welfare state" played by aid to widows of Civil War casualties and by veterans' pensions.[9] Beyond the classic distinctions between the Bismarckian and the Beveridgian welfare state (see above), her analysis presents a fundamental historical dimension of the welfare state, and it is to that original *civic welfare state* that we must return when the insurance bedrock erodes. But that raises two difficult questions. The first is philosophical: what principle of justice can be the basis of the welfare state when a simple mutualization of social risks is no longer satisfactory? The second question is ostensibly more technical, but has broad repercussions: does the progression, or return, to an essentially more civic system not imply that we are progressing from financing based on social contributions to financing by taxation?

### Tearing the Veil of Ignorance

As we have already emphasized, the welfare state functioned under a "veil of ignorance," an insurance principle that presupposed the equality of individuals with regard to various social risks. The opaque nature of society was thus an implicit condition of the sense of equity. All members of society could be considered interdependent insofar as they perceived the nation as a relatively homogeneous class of risks. But this perception is ceasing to correspond with reality. We have already stressed the consequences of the progress of genetic medicine, but the phenomenon is more general: as society gains more knowledge of its differences, a considerable change in the perception of fairness tends to be produced.

Retirement pensions in France provide a simple example of this phenomenon. Life expectancies of various socioprofessional groups are now precisely known, thus allowing a calculation of the various time lags of recovery of contributions, that is, how much time of collecting a retirement pension is necessary to obtain a "virtual reimbursement" for the contributions paid into a pension plan.[10] The inequalities in this framework are very clear: individuals in the upper managerial level collect a pension for an average of seventeen years, as opposed to less than fifteen years for the clerical staff. This makes the relative loss of French confidence in their retirement pensions understandable: many people fear they will not benefit from them after they have paid contributions during their entire working life.

This increased knowledge of the differences between individuals and groups strains the bases of the social contract. If some know they will be spared some costly serious illness, will they agree to continue paying the same contributions for health insurance as those who are genetically condemned to develop that affliction? In an unpredictable universe, the essence of justice is *procedural*: it is bound up with the search for a universal rule. Our increased knowledge of inequalities and differences makes that definition of justice problematic. In John Rawls's work, the "principle of difference" (inequalities are acceptable only if they are beneficial to the most disadvantaged) is formulated only under a veil of ignorance. This principle is adopted because individuals must foresee that they themselves may be the most disadvantaged. But what happens when we know who the rich and poor are? The automatic adoption of the principle of difference can be questioned.

If I know statistically that I will benefit less from my retirement pension than others, why will I agree to pay contributions at the same rate as they do? I will consider it fair to take account of this disparity. I will want to replace a procedural equity, indifferent to variations in individual situation, with an *equity of results* that integrates those variations. This dynamic of knowing something about individual and group differences is not strictly limited to separating insurance and solidarity. First it undermines the bases of the insurance principle by reducing the size of the classes at risk. So long as the exercise of justice is linked to the demarcation of classes of homogeneous risks (in which the risks are the same for everyone), these classes will shrink as knowledge progresses. The insurance mechanism can still be applied to more limited groups, but this is no longer a system of social insurance. Insurance under a veil of ignorance aggregates and promotes social cohesion; but when available information on individuals increases, a trend of dissociation begins. Information promotes differentiation. In the extreme case, there would no longer be anything to insure if individuals could be infinitely distinguished, for no "population" could then be formed.

By the same token, relations between the notions of justice and solidarity are radically changed when information promotes differences. In other words, tearing the veil of ignorance means a return to the traditional opposition between distributive justice and commutative justice.[11] The classical welfare state has partly gone beyond this opposition, since social insurance combines a rule of equity with a mechanism of distribution. Solidarity can be defined as a form of compensation for differences, and hence is a positive act of sharing, while justice refers to the recognized legitimate norm of this sharing. In insurance under the veil of ignorance, justice and solidarity overlap: sharing risks is both *a norm of equity* and a *procedure of solidarity*. Equity and redistribution are then merged. This is no longer the case when the veil of ignorance has been torn and the notion of justice is once again problematic: what is just is no longer definable a priori when the differences among individuals are no longer random.

Thus, we are entering a post-Rawlsian age of thinking about society. Rawls's *Theory of Justice*, based on a principle of justice formulated under the veil of ignorance, presented a theory of the type of welfare state that is currently being obliterated. What we need now is an approach of justice under the curse of knowledge of the differences among men.

## Justice and the Knowledge of Differences

The progress of our knowledge of human inequalities leads us to distinguish three factors of differentiation: natural differences, behavioral differences, and chance. The question is: if the role assigned to chance has diminished, how can a legitimate principle of solidarity be established, since it can no longer be a purely procedural principle of equality? Solidarity is now based on the differential treatment of individuals and can no longer be derived from the application of a fixed and universal norm.

One aspect of the issue is to determine a position with regard to *natural* inequalities. If equity consists only of the equal treatment of individuals, those natural inequalities only concern us if the principle of equality of opportunity is adopted. In this context, solidarity is defined as an act of compensation for natural inequalities, and becomes the source of contemporary sensitivity to *discrimination*.

The dominant concept of reducing inequalities often appears as a response to discrimination, in the broad sense of differential treatment of individuals because of their *natural* characteristics (sex, age, race, physical or emotional handicaps). The struggle against discrimination is a new way of connecting a norm of equity (the equivalent treatment of individuals) to a policy of correcting differences.

Can justice obliterate the real importance of nature? This is not the same as fighting discrimination, but would go much further, to the utopia of a human re-creation of nature according to a radical principle of equality. But clearly, such an approach leads to the dead end of totalitarianism. Can we find a space between the totalitarian utopia of eradicating natural differences (intelligence, heredity, family background), on the one hand, and submitting blindly to its dictates, on the other?[12]

This is what the notion of *handicap* attempts to convey. It refers to a form of natural physical or mental inequality that might be distinguished from other disparities between men without turning them into objective entities. Neither medicine nor science in general has any facts in this category, except for the belief that the "normal" man can be defined. A handicap can be developed only socially or politcally. Justice in the correction of natural inferiorities is thus to be constructed socially, for it cannot be based either on a principle of procedure or on a merely scientific category.

Differences related to *behavioral* variables emerge more easily from the area of equity. If disparities result from the voluntary action of men, they are accepted by the same token. Thus, ever since Locke, liberalism has justified differences of wealth resulting from activity: someone who has not worked hard cannot find it unfair that someone who has labored diligently has gotten richer. The equity of a compensatory act stops at the gate of individual responsibilty. But this clear expression of the limits of solidarity is problematic, for two reasons. First, because the relation between responsibility and will is not always simple. Responsibility is a moral category, clearly identifiable in a legal sense, while will is a pyschological category. Lack of will is complex to analyze. The whole history of modern individualism is permeated by a contradication between recognition of the individual and the observation that he is divided, part stranger to himself, inhabited by an unconscious he does not control.[13] But even more broadly, what remains problematic is the distinction between the sphere of the innate (the givens of nature) and the sphere of the acquired (that of individual responsibility). The argument about justice is largely a debate about the dividing line between what pertains to the behavior of individuals and what refers to their innate handicaps.

Thus, it is impossible to find a purely procedural theory of justice equivalent to the insurance principle once the veil of ignorance is irreparably torn. Nor can we hope to devise a quasi-mathematical model of justice by developing the idea of equity based, for example, on responsibility toward future generations. All that remains is a political and circumstantial approach to justice. Once we are no longer satisfied with the most minimal definitions on which a welfare state could be constructed (the equality of law), we must conclude that there is no possible theory of justice. Justice is always uncertain, derived from the public debate in which the social contract is patched together. Hence, beyond undermining the insurance system, tearing the veil of ignorance also has a profound impact on our view of politics, especially its relation with law.

The political system claims to be a system of law, for it intends to institute a universal norm. Laws are made at a distance from concrete individuals and intend to encompass general human nature, and this is the basis of their legitimacy. But this is no longer the way things work. Political regulations must now be made with knowledge of their target population, which means that the practice of politics is increasingly confused with the search for justice and grows more remote from a simple, passive management of the rule of law. Hence, the new conflicts that structure our society are no longer simply conflicts of redistribution, in a traditional perspective of the class struggle. They are increasingly *conflicts of interpretation* about the meaning of justice.[14]

Several social conflicts in the last ten years have demonstrated that the notion of justice or equity prevails over that of interest. This is not pure rhetoric, a way of concealing a selfish interest behind a noble value, but goes much further. It signals the entrance into a new age of society, where the individualist imperative of equality before the law tends to prevail over the notion of defending collective interests. The management of conflicts today is part and parcel of an effort to find a consensus on the categories of justice. This was obvious, for example, in the great dispute of the French truck drivers in 1992, who were protesting the injustice of granting the same number of "points" on drivers' licenses to professionals driving one hundred thousand kilometers a year and to amateur drivers. The Rawlsian principle of equality in the distribution of primary goods was rejected in this case. The stakes of the conflict were to find a formula of "equitable difference." These conflicts of interpretation about the meaning of justice are now at the center of social and political life in more and more countries, complicating traditional debates about economic redistribution.

## Solidarity and Deliberative Democracy

Is it possible to restore the opacity that would make it easier to manage social issues? Some dream of that today. In the 1960s, man saw the increased transparency of people and things as the condition for a calmer democracy, as a way of moving from an irrational, opaque universe to a world of rational discussion. Modernist democratic ideology made information the condition of social peace, implicitly assuming that conflict rested ultimately on simple misunderstandings. Thus, the French CERC (Center of Studies on Incomes and Costs), for example, was established to provide objective bases for a comprehensive income policy. Democracy and transparency were thought to work in tandem.[15]

Things seem more complicated now. Every day produces evidence that social protest is stoked primarily by information designed to extend the field of reference of individuals, allowing them to look ever farther into their neighbors' gardens, and thus to evaluate their own situation more precisely in comparison with others. In a complex society, the relative positions of various individuals and groups are always subject to discussion. As long as society is perceived simplistically, as structured into classes assumed to be homogeneous, the issue of justice can be formulated globally. But when that condition disappears, society appears as what it is: an unstable tangle of individuals and multiple economic, social, and professional classifications. When ideology declines and information on real situations increases, the discussion of the relative positions of both is extended.

There is an increasing trend of "publicity" that complicates and reinforces the exercise of democracy today. A more transparent society is more unstable and vulnerable. Transparency can become a trap, but it cannot be avoided when the political order is no longer thought to conform to nature, as in ancient societies, or to law, as in early modern society. Henceforth, the production of solidarity and the invention of a deliberative democracy go hand in hand, and therefore the old oppositions between formal rights and real rights, political rights and social rights, as well as the difference between the democratic idea and the socialist idea, can all be transcended. From now on, social rights and political rights can be rethought *together*, within an expanded theory of democracy.

The old opacity that was a condition of solidarity cannot be recreated artificially. However, we can try to distinguish two kinds of knowledge: the knowledge mutually available to citizens about one another, and the knowledge possessed solely by large organizations or by the state about its citizens. Thus, social transparency and individual transparency can be separated, even though the boundary between them is imprecise. In the broadest sense, social transparency is inherent in the very logic of modern society. But that is not true of individual transparency. If democratic society is based on the freedom and autonomy of persons, it must preserve their privacy, leaving them closed to other persons in a certain way. In this case, democracy is linked to maintaining an *opacity of individuals*, where the protection of freedom is allied with transparency and solidarity. (This is demonstrated by the rules governing the information insurance companies can collect about their clients.)[16]

## *The Temptation of Social Victimization*

Reconstructing a new welfare state based on an imperative of civic order is not self-evident. It implies a stricter conception of social debt and a reinforcement of the sense of community membership. This is a difficult perspective to integrate into liberalism. Hence another model has emerged, whose dynamic is quite visible in the United States: this is the society of generalized compensation. In this case, social redistribution is not based on the recognition of social rights, strictly speaking, but derives from a radicalization of civil rights. Social results are expected not from the reinforcement of the national bond but from the strengthening of individualistic logic, and here a very broad notion of compensation for damages serves as a substitute for a political exercise of solidarity.

In a society of generalized compensation, the central figure of social interaction is the *victim* and not the citizen. There is an attempt to bring about redistribution through a concept of indemnity. By radicalizing the principle of commutative justice somehow, we think we can realize an equivalent of distributive justice. By being recognized as a victim, an individual can claim compensation. Hence the tendency to keep extending that category of victim. If one cannot hope for much as a pauper or a disadvantaged person, one must establish a claim to be a victim to improve one's situation. Originally, the notions of victim and indemnity were purely civil, pertaining to the classical law of responsibility; but they have ultimately come to constitute the central social paradigm in certain countries, and are even applied to whole groups.

It is not as citizens with a claim to social rights that minorities now seek to benefit from public grants in the United States; it is by promoting their status as victims—victims of a present injury, but also victims of a past injustice. This is what explains the constant reference to nineteenth-century slavery by the black community and the permanent emphasis on the threat of genocide or holocaust. The wounds and suffering of the past become a kind of capital. In this framework, it is the memory of inferiority and the dramatization of misfortune that constitute the perverse impetus of the demand for justice.[17] Thus, in 1989, the U.S. Supreme Court decided to compensate the children of the Japanese who had been interned in American camps during World War II, basing that decision on the fact that a specific population had suffered harm and should legitimately be compensated for it. In this case, the emphasis was not on an imperative of equality or brotherhood but on a demand for civil compensation.

In the United States, disadvantaged minorities and groups demand public aid as compensation for an injury suffered, and not as deriving from a right to a specific share of the national pie. Traditional social struggles for redistribution thus give way to a new type of conflict based on the intepretation of legal categories: from now on, the issue of social justice in the United States will be played out in the Supreme Court and not on the ground of class struggle.

In this case, going beyond the traditional welfare state produces a general "victimization" of society. Justice is perceived solely in terms of compensation and redress. The tremendous increase in the number of trials for civil responsibility and the individualist alternative to the welfare state are simply two sides of the same coin.[18] The notion of risk or misfortune no longer fits into this framework either. Every "accident" is ultimately ascribed to someone, a person or a "system." The propensity to tuberculosis in the black ghettos is cited as an example concerning a serious illness. A sociological analysis of chance can always be made, and an ersatz welfare state based on the figure of the victim must always denounce a guilty party. There must be no bad luck, but in every circumstance, a sociological or historical determination. Paradoxically, the liberal vision of compensation comes to rest here on an indeterminate extension of the Marxist analysis of the economic and the social. This kind of welfare state, shaped by radical individualism and the figure of the victim, thus marks an increasing deviation from what can be called the new political model of the welfare state.

In some sense, the United States is currently moving in the opposite direction from European countries. In Europe, as we said, the construction of the welfare state has been identified historically with the establishment of an insurance based on the principle of the socialization of responsibility (moving from the notion of fault to that of risk). This insurance has never existed in the United States, and even if President Clinton's health care reform plan advocated it momentarily, the basic trend of institutions and customs is not in that direction.[19] Even American liberals generally expect more from an extension of civil rights than from an assertion of social rights.

While it was already discernible since the 1970s, this tendency has become more pronounced with the emergence of a multicultural society. Liberal thought tends increasingly to emphasize the idea of autonomy: the basic principle of social life is giving each individual and each group the possibility of living according to its own principles and lifestyle. The central social values are tolerance rather than solidarity, and impartiality rather than equality.[20] The "good society" is the society that allows the peaceful coexistence of differences, not the society that guarantees inclusion. The principle of citizenship no longer implies a demand for redistribution in this framework, but is reduced to common trust in autonomy.

Ultimately, society is conceived on the old principles of the right of the people, when the people sought to define the conditions of peace between nations in the seventeenth century, that is, between separate political bodies. By the same token, the United States is being transformed into an assembly of quasi-nations satisfied to establish a simple modus vivendi.[21] It is thus the complete antithesis of the model that bases the renewal of the welfare state on the figure of the citizen.

## Remaking a Nation

The political life of democracy and its social life are increasingly identical. In a certain sense, the welfare state is becoming more directly political. Henceforth, the search for justice is an immediate resort to social arbitration and democratic deliberation, the search for a common path among a tangle of individual preferences, scales of values, and concepts. In a word, that search is an effort to speak the same language and to agree on the forms of the social debt. The welfare state must be rethought in connection with a conception of the nation as a space of accepted redistribution. Outside of that, in fact, there is room only for the minimal control of a guarantee of individual independences on which, on another scale, relations between nations are based. It is only in the perspective of a *substantial solidarity* that the welfare state can be constructed, and without that, the very idea of a nation could exist only as an archaic species.

The Canadian example is illustrative in this context. In Canada, it is the welfare state that has preserved the sense of national cohesion at a time when the federal bond seems politically fragile. The welfare state there served not only to guarantee the benefit of collective wealth and to reduce the tensions of industrial society, but it also helped integrate the regions into society. Some observers have even attributed the failure of the 1980 referendum on Quebec sovereignty to the bonds that connect each Quebecois to the welfare state: the experienced bond of social involvement and solidarity was stronger than the political and cultural sense of separatism.[22]

The welfare state cannot currently be preserved without "remaking the nation" in some sense, that is, without revitalizing the civic foundation for mutual social debt. This helps to explain the difficulty of instituting a welfare state in some Third World countries. If an insurance system cannot be instituted without economic development and a generalization of a salaried class, the flaw of a solidarist welfare state is primarily due to the superficial character of the collective identity. When the sense of nationhood derives mainly from the individual appropriation of prestige symbols (identification with athletes or stars, for example) or when it proceeds from a simple opposition to a third party, it does not allow the establishment of mutual obligations. The nation is then understood solely on the model of an idealized bloc, assumed to be unified and homogeneous, but not as a space for redistribution. It is perceived as a fact, when it is only in the process of being constructed. The populist perversion of the idea of nationhood results from this ignorance of the democratic-solidarist dimension of democracy. The unity of the people is promoted by intensifying the rejection of the foreigner in order to avoid working out the terms of the internal social debt.

Along with emancipating itself from the sphere of labor and proving to be more "open" in one sense, the welfare state can also become more "closed" in another sense: the advances of solidarity can go hand in hand with a clearer distinction between native and foreigner. The political space of citizenship is, in fact, determined and rigid, while the economic space is variable and flexible. Eventually, that poses new problems for our societies. One's nationality made no difference for the allocation of allowances when those constituted the counterpart of income deductions on labor. But what will happen in the future with a system of benefits based less on the logic of a return of contributions? The question has not yet been posed.[23] During the debate on the institution of the Social Minimum Benefit (RMI) in France, for example, this issue was not seriously discussed. Hence, there is a definite risk that a brutal "nationalist" reaction will emerge someday, provoked paradoxically by a sharper awareness of the social bond. Thus, progress in solidarity can evoke a certain archaism. In ancient Rome, for example, the right to the *frumentum publicum* was strictly bound to the right of the city, and only a full citizen could take advantage of those food distributions.[24] In the future, vigilance will be necessary to insure that the expression of solidarity is not accompanied by the perverse stench of a narrow nationalism.

European societies today are characterized by contradiction. On the one hand, they need to remake the nation, to turn inward to reinforce the bonds of solidarity; on the other hand, they must open themselves outward economically. In some sense, both more and less are required of a nation: more of a "social nation" to reinforce the political cement, and less of an "economic nation" to develop the economy. The two imperatives are not easy to reconcile, as indicated by the tensions that surfaced during the ratification of the Maastricht Treaty. Yet both must be met at the same time.

## Dramatizing the Social Contract

We need the "moral equivalent of war," William James stated at the beginning of the century, deploring the rise of selfishness and incivility in the society of his day.[25] Only in this condition, he concluded, can America recover power and cohesion. Historically, as we have seen, part of the welfare state was connected with the war and was not engendered solely by the growth of the "Thirty Glorious Years." For if that period enabled the subsequent development of the welfare state in France, it did not lead to its institution in the West in 1945. It was, in the words of that time, "the spirit of brotherhood and the reconciliation of classes" that marked the end of the war and that produced the new forms of the institutionalization of solidarity.

Must we provoke a return to that "moral equivalent" today to reestablish the welfare state on a more solidarist base? As Michael Walzer recently wrote, "Defenders of the welfare state . . . seek to institutionalize and perpetuate the helpfulness born of collective crisis, the spirit of mutuality that arises among citizens confronting a flood or a storm or even an enemy attack."[26] But how can that be achieved? In the 1960s, people tried to recreate that spirit by talking of a "war on poverty." Today, the war against unemployment is sometimes evoked in France to attempt to mobilize energies, or it is seriously hoped that a political speech will be termed "Churchillian." But this is merely lip service as long as private agreements and support of corporate interests easily prevail over the general interest.

Morally, our societies have become increasingly schizophrenic, creating a peaceful coexistence between compassion for world poverty and the fierce defense of established interests. This is produced by the deterioration of the specifically civic space, which no longer provides a sufficiently strong structure for solidarity. By the same token, the sense of solidarity has trouble expressing itself coherently between the very close and the very distant, as we see in the development of recent "humanitarianism."[27] There can be no solidarist welfare state without a reconstruction of the civic sense as a sense of belonging to a common world. It is not only mobilization that is lacking; it is also its substratum, that is, the nation.

It will be impossible to recreate solidarity without finding a new collective cement. The problem is that the loci of ordinary public-spiritedness— military conscription, the school, even the neighborhood—are progressively disintegrating. The institutions through which the individual could once identify himself with the nation have become more fragile and more banal. How to remake a nation in these conditions? How to recreate a civic space? Where there is no military draft, as in the United States, some people hope to re-institute the system.[28] Can we dream of the revival of an ancient martial and fraternal public-spiritedness? Probably not, for that age is past: we will not return to a society that was considered communitarian, and the nature of individual identification with the nation has clearly changed. Utility and compassion have been substituted for the old notion of sacrifice. Where military conscription does exist, it is often challenged.[29] In individualistic-democratic societies, the masses are less willing to die for the homeland, as underlined clearly by the attitude of public opinion in the major conflicts of the late-twentieth century. The civic sense no longer proceeds mainly from self-effacement, but is expressed in a more complex way. Henceforth, the sympathy described by Adam Smith in his *Theory of Moral Sentiments* and the social debt developed by Rousseau can no longer be separated, as indicated by the favor enjoyed by the idea of *national service*.[30]

The moral equivalent of war cannot be decreed: more mundane ways must be tried to remake the nation today. Yet to progress, the social contract will have to be dramatized. That is one of the essential functions of politics, whose task it is to contribute to shaping the social bond by making it more visible.

## CHAPTER 3

# New Forms of Solidarity

THE DECLINE of an insurance society does not mean that the idea of social insurance is about to disappear. Insurance procedures cannot be ignored and will always constitute one of the modern forms of strengthening the social bond, but their role will be less central. They can no longer be either the main technique for encouraging solidarity or the main philosophical mode of representing social cohesion. Since the pendulum is not about to swing back to the idea of social citizenship, a progressive shift toward taxation for part of the financing of the welfare state is inevitable, even if health and social expenses are controlled better in the future.[1]

## From Coverage to Taxation

This shift to taxation will be accelerated by two factors. First, the disparity between the number of contributors and the number of beneficiaries must necessarily increase, not only because of unemployment but also for profound sociological reasons, such as the growing number of students, the increase of single-parent families, etc. The number of individuals who are socially autonomous, but economically dependent, is constantly on the rise. The process is accelerated especially because of economic factors. For example, to encourage employment, the French government has entered into a pernicious spiral of exemptions, which have become ends in themselves.

Second, there is general agreement that the cost of unskilled labor must be reduced in order to wage an effective struggle against unemployment. But since there is a consensus in France against reducing the net minimum wage, the cost of labor must be cut through a more or less broad exemption from making social contributions. Because those working at the guaranteed minimum wage (SMIC) currently represent 8 percent of the French work force, such an operation would produce an enormous imbalance in Social Security accounts, and could only intensify the demand for taxation.

Thus, everything is converging to raise the issue of progressive taxation for social expenses—illness, unemployment, and all cases of disability. (The issue of retirement pensions must be treated separately.) Diverse elements have combined to bring about this reorientation, which began in France in 1990 with the adoption of the Supplementary Social Security Contribution (CSG). For the first time, a deduction based on income and designed to finance Social Security was openly instituted in a long-term structural perspective. Ever since its inception, the sponsors of the CSG have considered it a pathbreaking move toward an alternative mode of financing social contributions, and not merely as a means to fill a temporary deficit. In the autumn of 1993, the French prime minister, Édouard Balladur, also called for a tax to finance Social Security. The issue is now clearly registered in the political agenda.

This development will not be easy. First, it collides head-on with labor union interests. The various organizations forming the global system of "social security" are controlled jointly by the "social partners," that is, the workers' and employers' organizations. Working together, this joint management represents an achievement judged essential by French labor unions, both because of the material conveniences it offers (reclassifying paid officials, for example), and because of the legitimation it grants the unions. Any kind of taxation would undermine this position, putting the French Parliament at the center of the game, since Parliament debates and votes on taxes. Of course, at present, the power of the social partners is only a façade, since it is in fact the government that reserves the power of final decision. But the transfer of legitimacy would have a strong symbolic effect. Social Security in France would no longer be a matter of "social partners," but a matter of all citizens, represented by Parliament.

But is such a transfer politically feasible? Even if we admit that financing social protection through labor-based contributions has reached its limit, the turn toward taxation is not very easy. Since aversion to taxes is already strong in France today, is it feasible to consider a transfer, if not a supplementary increase in rates? Are we not moving inevitably toward a generalization of the "fiscal crisis" of the welfare state in France, as experienced by other countries in the 1970s?[2] It would serve no purpose to glorify the image of the citizen if that of the taxpayer were to give way.

The transition from social partner to taxpayer cannot be handled simply, and two illusions must be avoided. The first is the technical one of thinking that clearly separating the fields of insurance and solidarity is sufficient to resolve the issue, since the cost of encouraging solidarity is reduced when it is better circumscribed. The second is the political one of believing that an overall fiscal reform would unite justice and efficiency through rationalization of the tax structure. Before commenting on the practicable forms of encouraging solidarity, we must clear away these two illusions.

## The Insurance/Solidarity Distinction

Both management constraints and philosophical uncertainties cooperate to make the notion that insurance and solidarity must be separated so widespread. Some see it as the preferred means of stemming the increase of health expenses; for others, the confusion of insurance and solidarity is the source of the legitimacy crisis currently afflicting the social protection system in France. Moreover, institutional realities are weighty factors in justifying such a separation. There are also social partners who are anxious to preserve their roles in the management of the social system, and have begun calling for a clear distinction between social protection based on a logic of insurance, which they would still manage, and a concept of universal minimal social protection, which would fall within the state's domain. The reform of French unemployment insurance in 1984 was a step in that direction, as was the creation of a solidarity fund for old age a few years later.[3] Yet many ambiguities lurk beneath the surface of this distinction.

In order to contrast insurance and solidarity, the values and techniques of management must be clearly distinguished. Insurance is a technique, while solidarity is a value. Thus, they are not antithetical: insurance is also a mode of encouraging solidarity. On the other hand, the financing of social insurance can fit into varied systems: it can be used strictly to produce solidarity. So then why is the insurance/solidarity distinction so popular? Aside from the factors already mentioned, it also has a utopian element. It promotes the idea that the spheres of society and politics, the market and citizenship, commutative justice and distributive justice might all be clearly separated. But things are never really quite so simple.

In a certain sense, everything in economic and social life is redistribution. There are no pure exchanges, on the one hand, or pure redistribution on the other. Even the retirement pension by capitalization, for example, is a form of redistribution, and not solely a function of decisions by the investor. If I invest at the age of fifty, it is not my decisions that will determine the result of the investment but the economic activity of future generations. Even if efforts are individualized, their results always have a social dimension.

Therefore, we must be careful not to adopt a dogmatic view of the distinction between insurance and solidarity. The search for a simple division of responsibility between the state, which is responsible for financing solidarity by taxation, and social partners, who would assume the management of the expenses of insurance, must not lead to a hard and fast separation of these two terms. As we have already emphasized, sufficiently, the interpenetration of the two orders has in fact been increasing, a process that can also be explained by economic theory.

In the jargon of social protection, the rule of contributivity is equivalent to the rule of "actuarial neutrality" in private insurance, which prescribes for each insured person the proportion between the benefits obtained and the premiums paid. But this rule of contributivity is far from clear, and comes up against two types of objections. On the one hand, there is no argument of economic efficiency that prohibits redistributions among categories of insured persons; on the other hand, the distinction between insurance and redistribution rests on a purely conventional typology of random states of nature.[4]

It is possible to move from an insurance view to a solidarity view according to the accepted criterion. As for retirement pensions, for example, the strict rule of contributivity implies linking the sum of the pensions to the updated salaries of an entire life. The simple fact of choosing the ten best years as a reference biases the contributivity. (Career trajectories are very different: some people experience an increase of their remuneration at the end of their professional life, while others stagnate.) Moreover, the type of hazard taken into account—life expectancy—can be modified by expanding or shrinking the target population. For the economist, insurance is thus only one particular method of redistribution and solidarity. "Actuarial neutrality" and "civic solidarity" are distinguished only by the types of risks and the methods of realignment. The current problem, then, is not so much contrasting two techniques as if they characterized disparate spheres but, rather, perceiving the general and multifaceted process that leads to an overall modification of social solidarity.

### The Great Fiscal Upheaval

The income tax has always been at the center of the left's political imagination, particularly in France, where its establishment in 1914 was preceeded by twenty years of bitter parliamentary battles. Since then, the transformation of the income tax has represented reform par excellence for socialists who lacked the power to revolutionize the economy directly, and hence hoped to change society through a redistributive income tax. Lacking a great political upheaval, they dreamed of a great fiscal one. Increasing the higher rates of the income tax has been so central to leftist political programs for a century that the opposition between left and right might even be summed up in this issue. Although this view of the income tax as a central operator of reform is still very active, it was shaken severely in the 1980s, and, again, the French case is illustrative.

Until the early 1980s, the fiscal credo of the French left was simple. Technically, it was necessary to increase direct taxes and lower indirect taxes, which were considered more unfair because they were less distributive; socially, it was necessary to increase fiscal pressure on the upper classes and reduce it on the working class. The 1982 establishment of the wealth tax satisfied both those conditions, but was an isolated symbol.[5] When the French left came to power, it proved generally incapable of carrying out the great fiscal reform it had previously called for. While it extended the previous trend of exempting low incomes (65 percent of households had taxable income in 1980, and only 50 percent ten years later), it progressively came round to a policy of reducing fiscal pressure on middle and upper incomes. Paradoxically, the income tax in France eventually produced one of the weakest returns among all the industrially developed countries![6] This was due not only to concessions, or bureacracy, or a resigned conversion to liberalism. It resulted primarily from a confrontation with the facts.

The traditional concept of socialism was historically linked to a dualist image of society, contrasting the big and the small, the middle class and the proletarians, the capitalists and the working classes. Since the leftists did not think of real society in its complexity, they were unable to make an impact on it. The left was a prisoner of its own myths. By the same token, the left was not able to think of solidarity in a *practical* way. It moved silently from fantasy to reality, almost shamefully, without acquiring the means to get out of the fatal fluctuation between an outmoded ideology and a wavering pragmatism; hence the importance of the collapse of the myth of fiscal reform as a central agent of change in the 1980s, the most visible and illustrative expression of the exhaustion of the traditional socialist vision.

### The Danger of Exclusion

Long-term unemployment, new poverty, homelessness: for about a decade, the rise of exclusion has constituted the major social fact in France. By the same token, the "social question" has shifted from an overall analysis of the system (in terms of exploitation, redistribution, etc.) to an approach focused on the most vulnerable segment of the population. The struggle against exclusion has attracted all the attention, mobilized energy, and evoked compassion. The new importance of charitable institutions constitutes one of the symptoms of this reversal. These organizations have contributed powerfully to reshaping the collective social imagination, dramatizing a great rift between two worlds that have always been considered homogeneous.

The exhortation to fight against exclusion has thus simplified our ideas about society too much, for the social dynamic cannot be reduced to the opposition between the "ins" and the "outs." Indeed, our understanding of society today is biased by the focus of all attention on the phenomena of exclusion, for even if it is the major social phenomenon of our day, it does not exhaust the social question. The denunciation of the poverty and misery of the world must not block a more comprehensive approach to the tensions and contradictions that permeate society.

Two other problems appear to be essential in France. The first concerns the general destabilization of the condition of wages. The multifaceted weakening of wage-earners (precariousness, flexibility) also alters our society profoundly and must be considered at the center and not only at the margins of society. As Robert Castel has stated clearly: "The most serious problem may not be unemployment. This is not to make the situation of the three million unemployed any less dramatic, but rather to demand that the degradation of the working condition be considered above employment."[7] This provocative warning is especially appropriate since it is certainly the weakening of this central mass that will ultimately fuel the increase in the number of excluded. We must keep in mind that exclusion is the result of a process, it is not a given social condition.

The second problem is what might be called "the question of the middle classes," and results from the growing rift between the logic of social policies, which concentrates increasingly on the world of the excluded, and the political and fiscal logic that makes the middle classes the pivot of social functioning. This is also the standard for evaluating the problems posed by the reconstruction of solidarity. The political feasibility of the move from the social insured to the taxpayer depends primarily on this issue.

### The Issue of the Middle Classes

In early 1990, the Democratic governor of New Jersey, Jim Florio, declared that the war against poverty was his top priority, and to wage that war, he raised the middle and upper rates of the state income tax and drastically reduced subsidies to schools in privileged districts in order to increase aid to the most disadvantaged segments of the population. A genuine revolt arose among the middle classes, who found themselves paying more to a state that was giving them less, and the Democratic Party was badly beaten in the next Congressional election. The story clearly sums up the new issue of the middle class in the United States during the last decade or so. A host of articles and books has been devoted to the problem, most of them considering that as the main cause for the decline of the Democratic Party during the 1980s.[8]

In their significant book of 1991, *Chain Reaction*, Thomas and Mary Edsall regard the transformations of the welfare state as the major vector of the political shift to the right in America.[9] They maintain that the strength of the Democratic Party has historically been linked to its capacity to embody a "progressive coalition" between the black population and a large part of the white middle class, a coalition cemented by a Keynesian philosophy of the state, inherited from the Roosevelt era. This coalition fell apart in the 1980s for a very simple reason: the Democrats had become increasingly identified only with "minorities" and seemed primarily to express the specific demands of those groups. By the same token, the party had tended to make general social programs secondary to campaigns targeted to specific populations, and hence had reached that "boiling point" of the middle class, which was fatal to the Democrats.

Are the problems posed in the same terms in France? The inflation of expenses in that country also leads to asking the question of targeting social policies. However, two very different spheres of social policy must be distinguished here: that which pertains to the insurance-solidarity system, and that which concerns systems of social aid. The perception of their relationship is not the same as in the United States. In the United States, the notion of the welfare state alludes mainly to social aid, while in France it refers mainly to the system of social insurance (hence, the term "welfare state" is not completely applicable, *stricto senso*). In France, it is hard to imagine a targeting of social coverage for health care: on the legal level, since it depends on a contributory principle, even if that principle tends to be diluted, but especially for political reasons, since it would inspire revolt in the wage-earning middle classes and would open the way to all kinds of risks.

The situation of social benefits is posed in different terms. Only some of these benefits are subject to means testing (family benefits or the parental benefit for education are thus paid unconditionally to everyone). But the number of benefits subject to means testing has been growing since the 1970s: housing benefits, family supplement, benefits for single parents, education benefits, benefits for young children. By the same token, an increasing number of households find it unfair to see themselves excluded from social or family benefits and consider themselves abused, if not disadvantaged, compared to more modest households which draw family supplements, housing benefits, educational benefits, etc. In this case, individuals do not evaluate the justice of the system (according to the principle and its intention), but rather its practical and individualized effects. It is

never the quantity of resources in general that is discussed, but the fact
that someone knows such and such a family whose situation seems com-
paratively "abnormally" favorable or unfavorable.

The question of solidarity must be reexamined with these facts in mind,
never forgetting that it is posed under a severe political and economic
constraint. Two paths can be explored: the increased selectivity of
benefits, and the redefinition of the structure of rates.

## The Selective Welfare State

Targeting social benefits is fashionable in most industrialized countries:
the general idea is that selectivity constitutes a solution to meet the financial depression occuring everywhere in the welfare state. A report of the
European Community published in 1993 on *Social Protection in Europe*
emphasized this development: "In time of depression, when resources are
scarce and needs are important, there is a great temptation to target more
the benefits of the neediest." A symbolic example of this development can
be noted in New Zealand. In 1926, this little social-democratic laboratory
was the first country in the world to institute a universal system of family
benefits. Since 1990, such benefits have been allocated only with means
testing.[10] The issue is now on the agenda everywhere. A growing number
of countries have developed benefits adjusted to revenues or subject to
means testing. Thus one of the fundamental dogmas of modern welfare
states, that of the universality of benefits, suffers a direct hit.

The universalist principle has historically been at the heart of the civic
and national conception of Social Security. The preamble of the French
regulation establishing Social Security referred explicitly to that principle:
"Social Security calls for the development of a vast national organization
of compulsory mutual aid which can be fully effective only if it presents
the character of a very broad generality both in terms of the persons it
includes and the risks it covers. The final goal to be achieved is the realization of a plan that covers the entire population of the country against all
the factors of insecurity." Universality was a way of organizing a symbolic
obliteration of class differences in a part of society.[11] Hence the centrality
of this principle in leftist rhetoric, consistent with the perception of social
benefits as rights.

This is why the left in France has always denounced selectivity, which
is accused of stigmatizing the poor and prompting a return to the moralizing age of assistance. The left has consistently demanded the abolition of
means testing and called for widespread access to benefits. This was stated
in 1970 (when the benefit of a single income was instituted), in 1974 (establishment of the school allowance), and in 1977 (introduction of the family

supplement). Giving to everyone through social benefits on the one hand, and taking from the wealthiest by taxation on the other, has been the consistent position of the left on this issue. The right, more pragmatically, has made do with advocating a "moderate social selectivity," setting relatively high ceilings since the 1970s for the allocation of most family benefits.

The rule of universality has existed up to now, yet it is currently being challenged with an economic argument:

> In a period of depression, the egalitarian welfare state can no longer be the model of reference, except for covering the heaviest medical expenses. If it is based on a uniform social excise tax, no matter what the income, it is unequal and generates unemployment; but if it is based on an equal treatment of all Frenchmen, it neglects the special needs of the lower classes and clashes with the rationing of resources engendered by the underemployment it itself has contributed to creating. The boom in expenses and the need to reduce the burden on low salaries now imposes a positive discrimination among Frenchmen by favoring the needs of the middle and lower middle class. Others, those with the highest incomes, will have to agree to contribute more and receive less.[12]

First of all, is this increased selectivity of benefits politically practicable? Does it not collide head on with that "issue of the middle class?" There is no single answer, for the problems vary by country. In the United States, where French-type family benefits are unknown, selectivity in fact aims at the bottom 20 percent of the population, and so middle-class grumbling reflects the complete separation between those who pay and those who receive. Clinton's strategy was to reverse this trend by introducing a national system of health insurance for large risks that would cover all Americans, a social reform with universal effects. Ever since that proposal was formulated, debate in the United States has revolved around the concept of the selective welfare state. For a while, the Democrats made the health insurance plan the symbol of their policy,[13] while the Republicans talked of the "universal fallacy" whose costs cannot be controlled.[14]

Selectivity has quite a different meaning in France, since the rather high ceiling of means testing means that a considerable part of the middle class receives various family benefits: 60 percent of families with two or more children benefit, for example, from the school allowance, and the lower half of the middle class receives a housing allowance. According to Nicolas Dufourcq, it is because French society is in fact largely covered by selective benefits that their loss can be felt so painfully. Exceeding the ceiling of means is to enter a social category defined by regulation as almost "privileged" and symbolically leaving the middle class.

This assessment is crucial, for it goes to the heart of the sociological simplification inherent in the principle of selectivity: that it cuts society, on principle, into two groups, the beneficiaries and the excluded. By the same token, this dividing line can be legitimate only if it isolates absolutely distinct categories: the privileged on top and the excluded on the bottom. The only two obvious forms of selectivity are either placing the bar very high or very low, thus always returning to the allegedly clear opposition of the rich and the poor, to a Manichean and caricatured view of society. But it is not really obvious, not only because there is a large middle class which is grouped together or separated at the option of the privileged group, but also because it is difficult to fix absolute sociological borders. Selectivity can easily be conceived by contrasting the position of a CEO with that of a welfare recipient. But it becomes more difficult if the comparison is between a worker earning the minimum wage and a welfare recipient, or between a household of married teachers with two children and a senior executive bachelor.

If there are some factors that account for part of the middle-class uneasiness, the discontent of that group in France has another, more technical origin, linked to the perverse effects produced by the random overlap of fiscal and social thresholds. The income tax schedule, for example, is set without reference to the ceilings of access to benefits.[15] An attempt at rationalization and clarification can thus contribute to establishing an adjusted selectivity for family benefits in France. But can an increased selectivity in social and family allowances be considered? For example, could we consider paying family allowances with means testing?[16] Financially, that would be a real savings. But such a plan would hardly be feasible unless a very high ceiling were set. If family allowances were abolished for the 15 percent of the wealthiest households (comprising, roughly, senior executives and professionals), the calculated savings would be 14 billion francs.[17] This is both a lot and a little, since it would represent less than 5 percent of the total family benefits. On the other hand, it seems almost impossible to introduce selectivity into compensation for health care, since the removal of the ceiling on contributions already produces a real redistribution. Therefore, the possible field of selectivity is quite limited, except for the most elementary social aid, connected, for example, to managing situations of exclusion.[18]

The selective distribution of social benefits ultimately comes up against a contradiction. To be economically effective, selectivity must set relatively low ceilings and thus exclude a good part of the middle class; but it is then difficult to handle politically. On the other hand, to gain easy social acceptance, selectivity must eliminate only a small fringe of the population (those for whom the intended allowances represent a very small percentage of income); but then the savings realized is very small. Hence, there are only two practicable options: either an adjusted selectivity as currently exists in France for most benefits (but it would be difficult to reinforce or extend it), or, on the other hand, a strictly targeted aid, oriented toward groups in distress.

However, we must not limit outselves to economic reasoning and lose sight of the fact that social benefits also have a dimension of citizenship. They constitute one of the expressions of the social bond, and in their own way, they are a form of equality. This symbolic dimension is essential, so some form of universality must be preserved for certain benefits, even if a reasonable selectivity is implemented. Beyond the unavoidable search for budgetary savings, there is a risk of turning selectivity into a philosophical principle, a retrogression amounting to reducing the welfare state to a system of assistance to the poorest (the right-wing version of the ideology of selectivity), or, on the contrary, reviving the myth of the rich who can pay for everything (the leftist version). Instead, the new pathways of solidarity must include a redefinition of its content and a reinvention of the rates.

### The Content of Solidarity

The shift to a system of solidarity primarily implies breaking with the implicit expectation of an equivalent, the organizing principle of social insurance. The practical consequences of this break can be enormous. The almost total exemption of state officials in France from payment of unemployment contributions, for example, is no longer justified when the insurance logic is abandoned. If solidarity consists of organizing the security of everyone, it implies compensating for disparities in status.

Moreover, it may be easier to get a consensus on achieving such a reform in stages than on increasing the income tax schedule. Disparities of status are equal to natural or inherited characteristics, an area where the material of solidarity is objective and indisputable. Temporary income disparities, which the income tax is intended to redistribute, are much more complicated, since they refer not only to classes (rich, poor, middle) but also to individual cases. Since anyone may experience variations of income as a function of age, efforts, or professional advancement, an increased tax rate corresponding to increased income is sometimes perceived as unfair, for it affects a personal situation, and seems to penalize an individual effort or reduce the effects of a deserved promotion. This sense that taxation depreciates individual responsibility is also at the bottom of fiscal resistance. When classes were stable and individuals were bound to their fate, the income tax was purely and simply the favorite instrument of social redistribution. But things become more complex in a mobile society, where individual differences involve factors of age, training, and individual investment, as well as fixed class positions. The notion of the reduction of inequalities looks different in this framework.

The form of contribution of solidarity will be accepted more easily if it is linked to objective or inherited factors. Hence, solidarity between the disabled and the healthy, the young and the old, between protected jobs and endangered jobs is much easier to justify than solidarity between income categories. If solidarity among income categories is certainly fundamental and can even be expanded to consider income flow or inherited situations (e.g., the wealth tax), in the long run it cannot constitute the only prop of redistribution, short of paralyzing it. The reinvention of the form of contribution included that expanded view of the subject matter and objects of redistribution. Between traditional insurance (redistribution within a given class of risks) and the classic income tax (redistribution of temporary income), there must be a new type of form of contribution that allows a redistribution in terms of an expanded perception of the field of differences and inequalities.

## Reinventing the Form of Contribution

If we can no longer believe in a great fiscal upheaval, can we still speak strictly of fiscal reform? The French example of the CSG (Supplementary Social Security Contribution)[19] should be considered, for in a short time it has worked a silent revolution. The CSG is currently a form of contribution that straddles two concepts and has a hybrid legal character. It has the form of a tax since it must be authorized by Parliament; but it also resembles a social contribution, strictly assigned to a category of benefits initially (family benefits) and collected by agencies that collect Social Security contributions. Yet the CSG constitutes a convenient instrument of transition, for it has the advantage of being accepted in principle now by a majority of the French.

Sooner or later, it will probably be the development and adaptation of the CSG that will serve to help finance health insurance by taxation, substituting for the impossible overall reform of the income tax.[20] Experts have calculated that a "health contribution" of 11 percent on the total of household income would allow everyone the same health insurance as the current general system.[21] This type of financing would allow compensation for current disparities, the rates of contributions varying for health from 18 percent for wage-earners in a bracket that includes between 1 and 3 percent for retirement pensions,[22] while non-wage-earners pay an average of about 10 percent. This also amounts to a CSG, which would have to be instituted eventually to contribute to the financing of unemployment compensation.

In both cases, along with the expansion of the base of contributions in relation to social contributions, the development of the CSG leads to a massive redistribution between generations. Retirees were the privileged group of the 1980s, under the double influence of demography and social measures (the considerable increase of the minimum age for retirement since the mid-1970s); as of the late 1990s, they will have to contribute more to the common expenses.

# PART TWO

# Rethinking Rights

## CHAPTER 4

# The Limits of the Passive Welfare State

THE WELFARE STATE functions like an indemnifying machine, compensating for losses of income (unemployment, illness, retirement), taking direct responsibility for certain expenses (health), paying various allowances with means testing. But confronted with unemployment, this leads to a paradox: on the one hand, compensation keeps increasing; on the other, unsatisfied needs multiply. One wonders why it is not possible to pay workers rather than to indemnify the unemployed, to transform passive expenses into active ones. In some European countries today, passive expenses represent about three-quarters of the total sum devoted to employment.

There is another paradox: through social transfers, a large part of the cost of labor serves to compensate for the partial or total exclusion from access to labor for a large part of the population.[1] In France, there are twelve to thirteen million persons who avoid poverty or financial insecurity by receiving almost 180 billion francs in various forms of social benefits. Thus, taxes on labor must constantly be raised, leading to a reduction of its volume, in order to take care of exclusion. This leads to a pernicious spiral we might call a *social deflation*: an increasing quantity of nonworking people are cared for by a decreasing number of workers.[2] With seven to eight million Frenchmen today living on the guaranteed minimum income, we have arrived at the "self-destruction of solidarity."[3]

## The Economy/Society Separation

The pernicious effects of the welfare state are often cited to explain its current deadlock, as in the document published in 1994 by the French OECD (Organization of Economic Cooperation and Development).[4] The OECD called for "new methods, better conceived, without the unforeseen and undesirable side effects of past social policies," and advocated a widening wage gap to stimulate job creation. The OECD also suggested keeping issues of equity out of the labor market and handling them separately. In other words, efficiency on the one hand, solidarity on the other. This distinction was one of the great slogans of the 1980s, and thus merits discussion.

These harmful effects must be defined more precisely. In brief, two pernicious effects can be distinguished: that of structure and that of separation. The former is the effect of an overly narrow approach to a problem. For example, unemployment compensation is set without any comparison with available wages, and disincentives to labor are not anticipated. The pernicious effect results from a simplistic analysis that focuses on only one aspect and neglects the complexity of interrelations and causality. Although this phenomenon has been studied thoroughly by social scientists, abolishing these damaging effects is not easy, since several contradictory principles can conflict in any given social system (e.g., unemployment and labor arbitration), or the agendas of various agents (the state and individuals) may be distinct.[5]

The deleterious effects of separation are different, and correspond today to the separation between the economic and the social: the search for economic efficiency, on the one hand, and the functioning of the compensation machinery, on the other. When social imperatives and economic demands need to be coordinated, they end up destroying one another. This pernicious effect is institutionalized today as the separation between the economic and the social, and it is often conceived as an imperative of progress. But that is henceforth the issue: pernicious effects are not always what they seem.

## The Dissolution of the Wage Contract

Separating the economic and the social has resulted in an increase in mass unemployment and long-term unemployment. Although we shall not analyze the strictly economic causes of the phenomenon,[6] we must demonstrate how the social transformations of the 1980s and 1990s accelerated it and exacerbated the pernicious working of the welfare state.

Mass unemployment radicalizes the process of economic modernization by dissociating the economic and the social, production and distribution, competitiveness and solidarity. Mass unemployment takes the distinction between economic activity and the passive welfare state to extremes, thus embodying the contradictions of modern capitalism and the individualistic society.

Jean-Paul Fitoussi has shown that the European economies of the 1960s and 1970s were governed by an implicit social contract that embedded a whole system of implicit "subsidies" between agents and that promoted employment.[7] Low interest rates initially allowed the distribution of a higher mass wage, which encouraged employment. But the most important element was a relatively narrow range of compensations, in accord with a *consensus* (keep in mind the importance of the hierarchy of wages in society and the protests of the early 1970s). The less skilled workers were subsidized, as it were, by the more skilled, and this was the logic of the French SMIC (the minimum wage of growth initiated in 1971, marking a break with the sweeping logic of the previous SMIG, the guaranteed minimum wage). The de facto limitation on high pay allowed businesses to hire more unskilled workers. Some Swedish economists even talked of a "wage of solidarity," while the American economist Martin Weitzman used the term "share economy."[8] Thus, there was already an implicit redistribution within the wage-earning mass. Referring to the Thirty Glorious Years, Philippe d'Iribarne sheds light on the "invisible social policies" of businesses.[9]

The same system functioned among generations. The young accepted lower entry-level pay because they knew their pay would increase throughout their career, while older workers were implicitly subsidized through the seniority system. Summing up these data, Xavier Gaullier noted correctly that the level of employability of individuals was linked more to forms of social compromise than to their utility value.[10] We might define this system of the 1960s and 1970s as the "virtuous circle of Fordian increase," which guaranteed a certain synergy between dynamic efficiency and equity.[11] In this context, the welfare state naturally fell within the category of insurance, and its cost resembled a consumption of collective services.

The combination of these conventions and subsidies progressively collapsed during the 1980s, breaking the previous social contract. The first symptom of that collapse was the increase of inequalities. The hierarchy of wages was clearly opened, either at the top or at the bottom, depending on the country. In the United States, the trend was double: low incomes regressed a great deal (the minimum wage did not vary in nominal terms for ten years, from 1981 to 1991, so that it was significantly lowered in real terms), and at the same time, high incomes soared.[12] In Great Britain, the median real income of the poorest 10 percent fell 17 percent in the 1980s. In continental Europe, although low wages continued increasing in real terms, the proportional increase of the highest incomes was much greater. In France during the 1980s, for example, the richest households (the highest tenth) constantly increased their share of overall income, and the intermediate categories saw their situation deteriorate.[13]

The second symptom was the rise of real interest rates. While countries like Germany or Japan were spared, the rise in France was intense. The social consequence of this rise was mechanical: when the payment of pensions increased, the share of other income categories, particularly wages, fell significantly enough to allow businesses to maintain their profit mar-

gin. Two figures sum up this movement: the share of wages in the added
value fell in France from 71 percent in 1981 to 63 percent in 1994. Since the
level of individual wages did not fall (except for part of the middle class,
as we indicated), the adjustment was made in quantities, that is, in the
reduction of the volume of employment.[14] Hence part of the previous wage
cost was transferred to the welfare state.

Generally, Western economies in the 1960s internalized a large part of
the overall social cost at the level of businesses, while the tendency of the
1990s has been an externalization of that cost. We have briefly mentioned
the forms of internalization: implicit subsidies between categories of wage-
earners whose pay was not linked to efficient productivity; redistribution
among generations through seniority. On the other hand, the new
system that has gradually emerged is characterized by externalization and
differentiation.

*Externalization* means that lines of efficiency and solidarity, which had
been at least partially connected, have become increasingly dissociated.
Efficiency has become solely the responsibility of business, while the imperative of solidarity now pertains only to the welfare state. The separation between the economic and the social also corresponds in this sense to
disjunction between the micro and macro levels. The great leitmotifs of the
1980s were "let everyone practice his own trade" and "unemployment
concerns all of society, not businesses individually."

*Differentiation* means that labor is no longer managed in overall terms,
with wage scales, centralized negotiations, etc. Instead, issues of productivity and organization are handled on an individual level: businesses try
to pay each worker according to his real productivity (in conformity with
the classical theory). The result of this double trend is a simultaneous
increase of inequalities and unemployment. Skilled wage-earners in a position of strength can maintain or even increase their advantages, while
the less skilled and those who have no power will be excluded from the
labor market or will be unable to return to it.[15]

The transformations of the productive system, the transition from as-
sembly-line production to a more flexible mode of production, not only
have an organizational and technical dimension, but also produce new
social relations. The current deadlocks of society do not originate in the
system of production, strictly speaking, but in the *social conventions* underlying it.

## The Radicalization of Modernity

If mass unemployment is the new form of redistribution between economic
forces assumed in our societies, the development of the welfare state
reflects the growing rift between the economic and the social accompany-

ing it. We thus must try to understand the contradictions of the passive welfare state in broader terms than usual, for these contradictions refer not only to an economic dysfunction but also to a radicalization of modernity as a process of individualization and rationalization.

The implicit social contract of the 1960s was founded on a form of "archaism" in modernity.[16] The balance between the economic and the social was based on the acceptance of a certain heterogeneity: the coexistence in a single productive function of workers with very uneven abilities, the presence of many little niches of weak productivity in businesses. Social cohesion was broadly linked to this embedding of the social in the economic, but the accelerated modernization of the 1980s and 1990s has destroyed this arrangement. By being more radically "modern," businesses have eliminated all those little pockets of protective archaism, while the welfare state has concentrated all those microsystems of implicit social protection, which were previously scattered in the productive system, by paying the cost of mass unemployment. Many inefficient or unskilled wage-earners, who were integrated into businesses, have become paid unemployed.

In this sense, the paradoxes of the passive welfare state refer to the very foundations of the social contract, which means that it is no longer enough to think in terms of indemnification or compensation for damages. We must shift from a logic of repairing the breakdowns of the social system to affecting the content of that social system. The problem is the stucture of the social system itself, not simply the treatment of dysfunction or the handling of certain categories of expenses.

Keep in mind that the welfare state developed historically in its insuring and indemnifying form only because society could not maintain a certain homogeneity by guaranteeing work for everyone. That is why employment is now at the heart of the challenge to the welfare state, for unemployment is the aggravated form assumed by the contradictions of economic modernity in our societies. Behind the almost technical discussion of the possibility of transforming the cost of indemnifying an unemployed worker into the wages of a laborer lies a questioning of the foundations of that modernity.

Beyond this observation, the strictly anthropological dimension of this crisis of the welfare state must also be emphasized. This crisis also corresponds to the inception of a new age of individualistic society: an age of an increasingly radical dissociation between the citizen as a member of the collective and the worker as a member of civil society. The result is a striking gap between a democratic principle of inclusion and equality on the one hand, and a productive principle of differentiation and exclusion on the other. Hence solidarity leads to a polarization of the welfare state, to the absurdity of indemnification growing separately and autonomously, divorced from needs.

*The Wages of Exclusion*

A major danger is currently lurking in our societies: the temptation to pay wages for exclusion. It arises out of the conviction that unemployment will be with us for some time and the recognized need for a minimal social protection net. It is often claimed that our societies are rich enough to pay the cost of exclusion, and hence there is a tacit consent to a growing split between the spheres of the economic and the social. This temptation to pay wages for exclusion appears in two forms: the model of the handicap and the model of the subsistence income.

During the 1960s and 1970s, the welfare state progressively paid for persons who were shut out of the labor market by a physical or mental incapacity, or for accident victims who wanted to return to the labor market. Devised to handle short-term breakdowns, the previous system of Social Security in France was not suited to deal with long-term situations. In France, an allowance for handicapped adults (AAH) was instituted in 1975, when it numbered 100,000 beneficiaries; twenty years later, it listed more than 500,000. At the same time, a compensatory allowance for adults with at least an 80 percent disability was initiated in 1979, and currently covers more than 200,000 persons. To some extent, these figures correspond to real social progress, for persons who were once condemned to poverty or who depended on the fluctuating generosity of social welfare offices have a recognized right and are guaranteed the means of existence. But the increase of handicapped beneficiaries also corresponds to a more pernicious phenomenon of assimilating into the handicapped category those individuals whose problems of social inclusion cannot be settled by social workers. A report of the French National Audit Office has recently denounced these practices.[17]

Aside from administrative blunders, diverting allowances for the handicapped in order to cope with other social problems reveals a profound trend: the establishment of a system of indemnified exclusion. Unable to reintegrate a certain number of individuals, we somehow end up assimilating them as "socially disabled." The category of the handicap is thus progressively shifted from the medical field to the social, even including workers who have not adapted to technological transformations.[18] The phenomenon might even be called "handicapology."[19]

Such a trend expresses a serious drift from the welfare state toward a destructive institutionalization of the separation between the economic and the social, making a society of indemnification the complement of a society of exclusion. The drift is currently most pronounced in the Netherlands. In 1967, when growth allowed planning an unlimited development of the welfare state, the Dutch government instituted a system of disability insurance (WAO) that was particularly attractive since it guaranteed up to 80 percent of the last salary; in 1976, another law on disability pensions (AAW) extended that coverage to non-wage-earners, setting a minimum of benefits at 70 percent of the minimum wage. Anticipated initially to guarantee resources for those who were injured on the job, these measures were ultimately applied in the 1980s to laid-off laborers who had trouble finding a job. When the maximum period of indemnification ended, the open-ended disability allowance replaced the unemploment allowance. Thus, in 1994, more than 1.2 million persons were receiving disability allowances (for six hundred thousand indemnified unemployed at the same time), that is, 17 percent of the work force![20] As of 1986, the only persons receiving a disability pension were working people in the 55–64 age bracket.

The disability allowance has been at issue in France since 1993. Multiple abuses of allocation have been denounced in the press, but this absurd situation of a record rate of disability for one of the healthiest populations in the world is not simply fraud, it is the culmination of a purely financial view of the welfare state as a machine for indemnification that must exclude individuals from the labor market in order to aid them. The inflated number of persons "unfit for work" comes from the legal definition of the term: "Every person unable to procure an income by adequate work equivalent to that of a healthy person doing the same work, as the result of an illness, a work accident, or a handicap, is recognized as unfit for work."[21] And by adequate work, the law means all work suited to the person's education and professional experience. Thus, disability insurance could become the natural transfer from health insurance and unemployment insurance.

Just as the category of unemployment was invented at the end of the nineteenth century, so the category of social handicap was invented in the 1980s, and for the same reason: to handle populations that could no longer be integrated normally into society.[22] But now the citizen loses morally what the beneficiary gains financially: a form of solidarity appears, but at the cost of discarding society.

## *The Deadlock of the Basic Income*

The idea of a basic income represents an attempt to reconcile assistance and civic dignity. It has appeared in recent years under various names—universal allowance, income of citizenship, basic income—and consists of paying every individual a basic income from birth to death, regardless of employment, income, or compensation, to cover essential needs, varying only with the number and age of dependent children.[23] Advocates of this measure see it as a way to deal with exclusion and poverty without establishing narrow insurance systems.

The fundamental justification of a basic income is both economic and moral. It stems from the observation that the production of wealth is determined not only by temporary labor and capital supplies but also by an inherited and indivisible social capital (the technical level, the educational system, the cultural tradition). The basic income can be considered an egalitarian distribution of the income from that fund.[24] The amount of such an income is hard to determine "scientifically" in the framework of the present analysis, but its anticipated level is decisive in defining its real nature. If it were on the scale of current family allowances in France, it would only reorganize traditional benefits in a new form and in a readjusted philosophical framework. If it approximated the French RMI (minimum social benefit), or even the SMIC (guaranteed minimum wage), it would be an effective form of redistribution of the national income equivalent to a sort of civic workforce. Its advocates have proposed an intermediate figure: fifteen hundred francs per month per person (roughly three hundred dollars),[25] accompanied by the reduction of various current benefits (unemployment payments, family allowances, various social welfare aids).

I consider the universal allowance to be the extreme limit of the society of indemnification rather than the herald of a new approach to society, representing the pernicious and paradoxical aspect of the end of the classical conception of the welfare state. The idea of a universal allowance is a symptom of the increasing separation between economic activity and solidarity, and of a surprising convergence between a libertarian and utopian-socialist viewpoints. For utopians, it expresses the civic foundation of the social bond and infers from it the right to an income not linked to work. But the universal allowance also has many champions among libertarians: for Milton Friedman, a form of minimum social income has the double advantage of establishing a security net (thus satisfying a moral concern) while enabling a completely free play of the labor market. If each individual is guaranteed a minimun, he can accept or be forced to accept a low-paying job. In the same vein, Ralph Dahrendorf has explained that the institution of an income of citizenship would increase the flexibility of the labor market by allowing a reduction in the minimum wage.[26] Thus, the welfare state is in the paradoxical condition of uncontrolled libertarianism: a social macrocontract legitimates the totally asocial functioning of the market at the microeconomic level, while uncoupling the search for efficiency and the concern for solidarity.

By radically dissociating the economic from the social, the basic income allows the issue of employment to be pushed into the background. "The battle for employment is a rearguard fight," according to the Association for the Inauguration of a Basic Income,[27] while Jean-Marc Ferry has written, "Inaugurating the universal allowance is surrendering a hard line on the anachronistic subject of full employment."[28] The vision of a "post-labor" society blends unambiguously with the dualistic view of a separation between the worlds of labor and charity. For that reason, the a priori generous perspectives opened by the idea of a universal allowance lead to a paradoxical reversal: the advance of social right ends up supporting exclusion.[29]

To go beyond the limits of the passive welfare state, this trend must be resisted. First, inclusion through labor should remain the cornerstone of every struggle against exclusion. Belonging to a community does not imply only a system of solidarity. More profoundly, there is also the principle of a *mutual utility* that binds its members. Beyond a certain "right to income," there is a "right to utility." Men did not fight for the right to be housed, clothed, and fed by a paternal welfare state, but mainly for the right to live from their labor, to combine their income with the recognition of a social function. So the general social contract cannot be completely dissociated from private labor contracts. Thus, progress demands reinventing the idea of the right to work, rather than shaping a right to income.

### *From Compensation to Inclusion*

Today we are economically and intellectually deadlocked, both by the poverty of our imagination and by financial constraints. We cannot escape either by a headlong rush toward something new or by continuing to let the passive welfare state develop on its own. First, we do not have the financial means. But even if we did, we would reach a dead end, since the increasingly sharp separation between the economic and the social would lead inevitably to the self-destruction of solidarity and an increasingly marked ostracism of the excluded. We can still postpone this chain of events by exercising better control over a whole series of expenses, for there is always a small margin to maneuver. But that cannot be a permanent solution.

Nor can we dream of a return to those "invisible social policies" that integrated part of society into the productive system, to that protective archaism we mentioned. This question, the center of political debate today, must be approached in terms of the problems of international trade and the consequences of increased inclusion into the international division of labor. This is the main root of the protectionist argument: for businesses to be able to hire less efficient individuals and recreate all that internal "little makework" that was abolished by the imperative of productivity, the external constraint must be relaxed.

The strictly economic argument regarding benefits from a reasoned protectionism will not be discussed here.[30] But the question can also be posed in sociological and organizational terms: have we gone too far in modernization, that is, in the separation of the economic from the social? If so, and the protectionist illusion is rejected, what can be done? Going backward seems hardly conceivable, except on a small scale. If the cost of labor is reduced, businesses might be able to hire more easily, but they will not then return to previous modes of organization and to those quasi-protected little pockets of jobs whose loss is deplored. On the other hand, the means of producing effects equivalent to that former mode of embedding the social in the economic must be sought.

The objective to be pursued today is to find a modern way of internalizing social concerns that will produce both economic modernization and reconstruct the social fabric, allowing us to be both modern *and* archaic at the same time. Our way of posing the problems has an historical precedent in the late nineteenth century, when there was an analogous concern with reconciling the protective virtues of the old corporatist system with the market economy. Émile Laurent, one of the major French social thinkers of the 1860s, explained it thus: "The great issue of our time is finding social guarantees to substitute for those destroyed by the Revolution and whose absence is emphasized even more by the industrial system."[31] The nineteenth-century solution to that equation was to institute the insurance society. What equivalent of that "invention of society" can we imagine today?[32] We must try to move forward on the basis of the idea of inclusion. The need to get out of the passive welfare state and the search for a new form of economic inclusion converge in the idea of a new type of employment, bound inseparably with an expanded reunderstanding of social rights.

How can we move from a society of indemnification to a society of inclusion? Only by reintegrating individuals into the sphere of labor can we break the vicious circle that makes the solution of the problem (unemployment compensation) contribute paradoxically to aggravating the problem itself (unemployment). However, the centrality of employment also stems from the fact that employment represents the only dimension of exclusion that can be affected by public initiative. The state can do next to nothing to tighten the familial and social bonds that constitute an essential variable of exclusion: unable to do the "societal," the state must thus double the "economic." In these conditions, it is not surprising that 63 percent of the French regard the creation of jobs promoted by the state as a top priority.[33] The problem is that the jobs are not made to order, just as unemployment cannot be declared illegal. But is there a path to a new mode of unemployment compensation that allows a way out of the vicious circle?

For ten years now, many new paths have been explored to transform the passive notion of compensation so that payment for idleness can at least be changed partially into payment for work. In all countries, from the JOB program in the United States to the employment-solidarity contracts in France, experiments have been tried along that line. We shall not list and discuss them here, but we must emphasize that the various procedures have almost always been marked by improvisation. That does not stem solely from the circumstances and conditions of public decision, but has a deeper reason that has to do with the principles themselves: those measures were fragile because they were not based on any coherent conception.

The task today is the philosophical clarification of this transmutation of indemnification into inclusion, and the return to the right to work. An historical detour may shed light on this point.

## CHAPTER 5

# The Right to Work: History of a Problem

To MOVE from an indemnification society to an inclusion society requires a reexamination of the right to work—not a revival of the utopia of 1848, but a more modest redefinition of the composition of the rights and duties in work and social protection. Because the social pact is originally also a contract of social inclusion, it makes sense that its forms and implementation have fueled political and legal investigations since the birth of the modern state. But in the last century, since the development and growth of the welfare state, the thread of these debates has been lost. But we must return to them if our thinking about social problems is to acquire historical depth.[1]

*The Revolutionary Moment*

In 1789, when the planned Declaration of the Rights of Man and Citizen was discussed in France, all sides agreed to recognize that society must help its members in distress. Public aid, it was said, was a "sacred debt." But though they proclaimed this right to assistance, the revolutionaries of 1789 did not separate it from another more fundamental element: the right to live from one's work. They regarded the right to assistance as only a substitute for that more essential right to be assimilated into society. As Guy-Jean Target noted, "The body politic owes every man the means of subsistence, either by property, by work, or by the help of his peers."[2] "Every citizen has the right to demand that society provide him with work or with help if he is disabled," Adrien Duport specified.[3] Almost all the members of the Constituent Assembly agreed that every man had to find a living through his work and that public aid was only a palliative. Thus a general system of inclusion was imagined whose real linchpin was labor: it was in terms of labor that solidarity and social interraction were initially conceived. Moderates and radicals were unanimous in affirming this principle during the French Revolution, and positions in 1789 and 1793 were consistant on this point. The law of March 19, 1793, has often been seen as one of the first expressions of the program of the welfare state: "Every man has the right to his subsistence by labor if he is able-bodied; by gratuitous aid if he is unable to work. Providing subsistance to the poor is a national debt." But that was, in fact, a formulation of the social problem that had been accepted as early as 1789.

The major question was how to institutionalize this principle. In the summer of 1789, Baron Pierre Victor Malouet called for the establishment of a system of "offices of aid and labor,"[4] and in a brief pamphlet that had a brilliant success, titled *De la nécessité et des moyens d'employer avantageusement tous les gros ouvriers* (On the Need and Means to Employ All Unskilled Workers Profitably), Pierre François Boncerf advocated that large works be implemented to employ idle workers. "The first creditors of the nation are the arms that demand work," he wrote.[5] The disastrous harvest of 1789 in France imparted an urgency to these plans since it produced a massive influx of unemployed workers into Paris. Less than two months after the capture of the Bastille, public powers thus began setting up construction sites to occupy that population: canalizing the river Ourcq, removing refuse from the banks of the Seine, various suburban developments, etc. Some analogous construction sites, defined as workshops of aid, were also opened in the provinces at that time.[6]

## In the Beginning: Constraint and Assistance

Responding to poverty by providing work rather than alms was hardly original: it had existed since the beginning of the sixteenth century, and was linked to the very definition of the modern state as a protector state. The idea that "the poverty of the masses is a fault of governments" is an integral component of political modernity, the logical consequence of a conception of the state as reducing uncertainty and protecting security. At that time, it was widely accepted that the King had to "give the means to live to his needy masses," according to a contemporary formula expressing the program of the protector state in an archaic paternalism. But the need to provide work to the poor was not considered a simple moral debt of society; it was fully embedded in a combined disciplinary and archaic view of society.

The idea was to employ classes that were potentially dangerous to supervise and reform, to make vagabonds and vagrants settle down. An order of the Parliament of Paris of February 1515 was typical in this respect, stating for the first time the need to give work to idle individuals.[7] But these idle individuals were not considered "unemployed," for economic inactivity and social criminality were not yet clearly distinguished. By the same token, offering work to the needy and quasi-forced labor were thoroughly confused; and, significantly, there were plans to shackle the poor, who were to dredge ditches, sweep streets, or repair the city walls. Hence, those measures could hardly be distinguished from four-teenth-century arrangements for the forced enlistment of "gens oyseux" (idle people) in public works.[8] In the seventeenth century, the General Hospital (founded in 1656) represented the peak of that repressive notion by locking up beggars to put them to work. English laws were just as strict: in 1547, a ruling of Edward VI even reestablished slavery for vaga-bonds in certain cases.[9] Putting beggars to work was initially a disciplinary measure.

The economic dimension of the treatment of poverty emerged only gradually. A pioneering work of the sixteenth century devoted to public assistance referred to it explicitly. In *De subventione pauperum* (On Assistance to the Poor), published in 1525, the Spaniard Juan Luis Vivès argued that the main measure in the struggle against poverty consisted of organizing work: "So that manufacturers will not lack workers and the poor will not lack workshops, the public authority should assign to each manufacturer a certain number of those who cannot have a workshop of their own."[10] Vivès even called for a public economy of employment. Speaking of the poor who might form an association to open a workshop, he wrote: "Like those to whom the magistrate will assign some apprentices, they will be entrusted either with the public works of the city, which are quite numerous; or with all the works to be done in hospitals, so that all the capital and interest which, on principle, were designated for the poor are used by the poor."[11]

A century later, the first economists (those who invented the term political economy and who were defined as mercantilists because of their pro-tectionist goals) supported putting unemployed people to work to increase general social utility.[12] However, it was not until the eighteenth century that recourse to public works to deal with poverty was considered primarily in economic terms, rather than moralizing and disciplinary ones.

In this period, the issue of public works also ceased to be considered from a social viewpoint, and began to be thought of in terms of individual rights. Thus the article on "Labor" in the *Encyclopedia* noted: "Every man who has nothing in the world, who is forbidden to beg, has a right to demand a living from work." It is in this vein that the funds of charity works were organized in several French regions in the 1770s,[13] and Turgot gave a considerable impetus to this movement with a regulation of 1775.[14] From then on, the notion of charity workshops was clearly distinguished from previous forms of quasi-forced labor. As one of the most important eighteenth-century studies of the abolition of begging concluded: "For a long time, we have been seeking the philosopher's stone: it is found, it is work."[15]

### The Experiment of the Charity Workshops

The idea of the charity workshops reemerged quite naturally in France during the Revolution. As soon as the Committee on Begging was established, it accepted the principle of assistance by work, perceiving the only real solution to poverty as the creation of jobs for able-bodied individuals condemned to idleness by economic conditions. Hence, it was important for good government to insure that the employment level was always linked to population increase. But the workshops, which were organized in France in the summer of 1789, soon posed serious problems of organization.[16] First, their directors were overwhelmed by the number of applicants: in a few weeks, the workshop in Montmartre went from two thousand to seventeen thousand workers. Within a short time, the workshops were unable to cope with discipline problems. By definition, there was no selection procedure: the only requirements for admission were to be at least sixteen years old and live in the place of work. The workers were badly supervised, many were unproductive, and a great many profiteers did not even bother to show up for work, coming only on payday. At the same time that a social right was asserted, its implementation just as quickly appeared problematic.

The workshops were criticized on all sides. Regulations were multiplied to remedy those problems, but failed to do so. The situation became so alarming that, on August 31, 1790, the French Constituant Assembly decreed the reorganization of all workshops, defining two new types: in some, the able-bodied were to do piecework, while in others, unskilled laborers were paid by the day. But in both cases, the wage was always to remain below the normal rate and a more hierarchical organization was set up. In the winter of 1790, a considerable sum (15 million livres) was allocated to these new workshops. But the previous malfunctions were not overcome, and the workshops were permanently shut down in the spring of 1791. Only the spinning workshops for women and children continued to function during the Revolution.

The improvisational conditions of these workshops were certainly an important factor in their failure, but the basic principles of the system were also at fault. The organization of the workshops as instruments for the eradication of begging implied a clear position on three issues: the paupers' obligation to work, the status of payment (salary or aid), and the legal meaning of the workshops (expressing the right to work and an obligation for public authorities). Thinking on each of these points wavered.

First, the problem of obligation, which was not new. Ever since the sixteenth century it had been central to policies for the abolition of begging. The distinction between the "true pauper," who deserved to be helped, and the "false pauper," who wanted only to sponge off society, was always an essential concern for philanthropists. Indeed, begging could be considered an offense only if everyone could actually find work. Hence the inseparably moral and economic importance of the charity workshops: the offer of work they presented constituted not only an economic response to poverty but also permitted a clear delineation of the social debt.

What is the right to public aid without the obligation to accept the proposed jobs? The plan for the extinction of begging, presented to the Constituant Assembly in January 1790 by La Rochefoucauld-Liancourt, adopted an unambiguous attitude on this point: "The duty of society is to seek to prevent poverty, to aid it, to offer work to those who need it to live, *to force them to do it if they refuse*, finally, to assist without work those who have been deprived by age or infirmity of all means of performing it. This is the meaning of that political axiom that every man has a right to his subsistence, and of that incontestable truth that begging is an offense only for one who prefers it to work."[17] Hence the famous formula: "If someone has the right to say to society: *Give me a living*, society also has the right to reply: *Give me your work*."[18]

Could this obligation have a legal foundation, so that every individual had to choose between "forced" labor as a sentence for the offense of begging and "free" labor done in a public workshop? Did the new right to assistance paradoxically risk producing a novel form of constraint for individuals? The public authorities of that period did not have real means to apply such principles (for example, sentencing beggars to hard labor, anticipated by the law of the seventeenth century, was not widely practiced), and this practical limitation allowed them to avoid plumbing the depths of the questions. The same happened with the charity workshops: it was preferable to close them for circumstantial reasons than to respond radically to the legal and philosophical queries created by their functioning.

Economically, the charity workshops paid wages lower than the market level, a practical way to avoid a massive rush of workers. But the status of that payment remained ultimately undetermined, vacillating between the classical notion of a salary (in payment for work) and public aid (compensation for a moral debt of society), as if the very nature of the activity was basically problematic, an intermediate reality between work and a job. As long as this appeal to work to fight against begging was considered disciplinary, the question did not arise. Work was clearly a *punishment*; its objective was to train men to behave rather than to provide a truly useful product. In the seventeenth century, the author of a study of *La Police des pauvres de Paris* (Policing the Poor of Paris) thought that work was instituted "more to prevent idle people from begging or stealing, and to make them more accustomed to working than the task they do."[19] But when the strictly legal notion of forced labor was obliterated, things became confused. Behind the uncertainty of the economic categories, the tension between the personal rights (freedom, autonomy) and the social rights of the individual (taken over by the collective) also emerged.

## The Paradoxes of the Right to Work

Could the state conceivably be obliged to provide employment to those who were deprived of it? In other words, could a *right to work* possibly be defined? At the beginning of the French Revolution, this was explicitly accepted. It was not so much the right to work that appeared problematic, as the conditions of its application. While all members of the Constituant Assembly agreed that the government should never give work except to those who were absolutely unable to acquire it, they clearly did not appreciate the impossibility of that undertaking.

The Committee on Begging expressed its perplexity on that point in a report of 1790:

> How can that absolute impossibility be identified with precision? Take a man who—if he could not rely on work provided by the government, would have looked for it no matter how far away—but certain of finding it nearby, appears, says he lacks work and he really does. Another man will avoid hard work; if he is sure of receiving easier work from the administrators he will ask for it. Yet another will refuse a job that would employ him for several months and guarantee him a reasonable salary, because he is sure of finding work whenever he wants it, and will wait until he is in dire straits to come and state his needs. The salary difference will be only a minor obstacle to all those unavoidable inconveniences; for laziness, independence, and the fortunate faculty of living from day to day have and always will have a great attraction for the common run of men. What means will the government have, however multiplied and however divided one may assume its means of administration, to distinguish real needs, those due to worsening circumstances, to misfortunes the worker couldn't have anticipated or repaired himself, from the pretexts that skillfully cover laziness and lack of foresight? We would have to make a detailed study of the interests of every individual, his behavior, all the little circumstances that can still influence his present situation. Is that conceivable? And, on the other hand, is it not obvious that such assistance, whose principle would be humanity and the encouragement to work, would have consequences contrary to its intentions, that work would necessarily lose its energy.[20]

The central paradox of the right to work was clearly perceived: determining the conditions of the beneficiaries risked producing a real control of behavior. In other words, the material security of individuals would require the establishment of a dangerous, state-controlling society. Although the Constitutant Assembly did not delve deeply into that aspect of social rights, it must be examined briefly. Unlike civil rights, whose only function is to increase the sphere of individual autonomy (hence their designation as rights of freedoms or rights of authorizations), social rights define the forms of society's debt toward individuals (hence their designation as rights of claims).[21]

The two characteristics of social rights are, first, that they have a cost, and second, that they apply to concrete individuals. The subject of the right to free expression is the abstract individual; the subject of the right to public assistance is the specific individual, defined by his economic and social characteristics. And like all social rights, the right to work also includes a subjective dimension, it implies taking account of behavior. Thus, the right to work is a *limited right*, that is, it is on the border of the concept of right. We shall return to that later.

Another problem is that it may be impossible to define a right to work that would guarantee a positive result (giving a job to all who want one). In the *Encyclopedia*, Turgot approached the question by expanding the notion of a right of freedom: "Every healthy man must obtain his subsistence by his labor. . . . What the state owes to each of its members is the destruction of the obstacles that would hinder them in their industry or disturb them in the enjoyment of the products that are the reward for it."[22] In other words, by extending the scope of individuals' freedom, the *equivalent* of the right to work can be guaranteed in fact. If state intervention creates conditions that promote economic activity, a right of claim and a right of freedom merge in work: work is then simply a question of individual will, since voluntary inactivity is virtually impossible.

This was how the Constitutent Assembly Committee on Begging justified the abolition of the charity workshops: "It is through a general influence that the government must act in the means of the work it must create: its intervention must be indirect; it must be the motivating force for work, but must avoid appearing to be, as it were."[23] This philosophy of public intervention that aims at substituting opportunity for a formal right does not only correspond to a procedural conception of state action; it also expresses a new subject: the collective. "The government must not be foresighted for each individual . . . , but it has the duty to be foresighted for all. Through its general legislation, it must provide the guaranteed means of obtaining work for all those who need work to exist," noted the committee.[24] Thus, there is a shift from an individualistic approach to a statistical one for providing work: "This large question can be usefully resolved only to the advantage of the largest number." In this framework, the very notion of right no longer has any meaning. Faced with the collective, the category of right gives way to the category of the state's duty of involvement.

*Assistance through Work*

Although the notion of the right to work was shunted aside, the idea of assistance through work as a positive alternative to alms remained widespread in the nineteenth century, even among liberals. The principle of the charity workshops still constituted a kind of insurmountable barrier for the social reformers and philanthropists of the period, who continued to express themselves in the terms of La Rochefoucauld-Liancourt. In his famous treatise, *De la bienfaisance publique* (On Public Charity), published in 1839, Gérando thus reasserted the superiority of assistance through work: "When an able-bodied pauper is not employed, or when he is not employed to his full capacity, he must be given help in the form of work, and only in that form. That principle is fundamental in the system of public aid. If society must assist the unfortunate, it owes nothing to the idle. The pauper who refuses work he is able to do, when that work is offered him, has no right to receive as aid what he could have derived from his labor. Not only does he then have no right to be helped, but all other aid must be refused him."[25] But obviously Gérando did not even consider fitting that social policy into the idea of the right to work. In many respects, he was much less daring than the Constituent Assembly. His perspective was mainly that of moralizing through charity, and did not aim at proposing a general policy or dealing institutionally with a social problem as a whole.

From this period to the end of the nineteenth century in France, by creating private charitable works, a whole paternalistic and philanthropic environment continued the idea of assistance through labor, which was practiced most often under the live-in system.[26] A host of local initiatives thus multiplied "workrooms," "refuges," "sanctuaries," and "hospices." From the 1830s on, however, one form of aid through labor created a special interest: the agricultural colony.

Between 1830 and 1850, the establishment of agricultural colonies triggered a philanthropic enthusiasm equal to that stirred by the workshops of aid in the eighteenth century. The first experiments had taken place in Holland in 1818 and were based on a simple idea: give able-bodied beggars uncultivated lands to clear and thus give them work and the means of subsistance, while relieving society of the cost of maintaining them. Organized as joint-stock philanthropic societies, the four establishments founded in Holland numbered almost twelve thousand persons twenty years later. The experiment was widely discussed in France, where Huerne de Pommeuse devoted a thousand-page book to the issue in 1832,[27] and Louis-Napoléon Bonaparte made it the key to his *Extinction du paupérisme* (Extinction of Poverty).[28] Some hoped this could provide for the needs of one or two million paupers.[29]

The agricultural colony placed the philanthropic and moralizing concern into the framework of a traditionalist vision of society, and hence it was enthusiastically promoted by Catholics and conservatives. Advocates of what was called Christian political economy distrusted industry and the displacement it caused, and saw agriculture as the real basis of work that was both moral and fertile, guardian of the family and the social structure. "In the present state of society, in France and in Europe, the only remedy to pauperism is found in agriculture," noted Villeneuve-Bargemont, one of the most influential economists of the period.[30] Achievements in France, however, were limited and only those colonies that accepted mostly juvenile delinquents had much success (the most famous of them was Mettray, near Tours, where Jean Genet was one of the last boarders in the twentieth century).[31]

In the final analysis, these various experiments involved only a small number of persons, even if they did play a central role in the social imagination of the period. Their only institutional importance was as prisons, where work was considered one of the major vectors of moral rehabilitation; and many institutions of a mixed nature, accepting both beggars and criminals (like the colonies in Holland) also emerged. But the Revolution of 1848 was to place a more radical type of investigation on the agenda.

## *The Debates of 1848*

On February 26, 1848, a decree was posted on the walls of Paris: "The provisional government of the French Republic promises to guarantee the life of the laborer with work; it promises to guarantee work to all citizens." The hand of the provisional government was forced by Louis Blanc and his friends. Two weeks later, the famous national workshops were opened with no planning. Numbering only a few thousand men at first, they counted almost one hundred thousand just before the June events, which were to sound their death knell. The experiment was such a monstrous failure that no one later claimed paternity for them.[32] Furthermore, the workshops were the object of violent criticism right from the start. The left accused them of embodying only an insipid and degraded form of the right to work. Louis Blanc and his friends advocated establishing cooperative production workshops to dispossess capitalists. In any case, they made sense only in terms of progress toward socialism, as François Vidal explained in *Vivre en travaillant* (To Live by Working): "The right to work, whether we know it or not, necessarily implies the organization of work; and the organization of work implies the economic transformation of society."[33] The right wing denounced their lack of discipline, their low output, and the many abuses they produced, even if they admitted that the workshops had made it possible to deal with high unemployment and to curb the workers' demands in the spring of 1848.

Yet, the failure of the workshops did not immediately discredit the idea of the right to work. Paradoxically, the subject became the crux of the social and political debate during this period. (Prior to 1848, only Lamartine and Victor Considerant had developed the idea.)[34] The first major discussion of the right to work, which had been outlined only fifty years earlier, took place during the preparation of the constitution of 1848.

The first draft of the constitution, read from the rostrum by Armand Marrast on June 20, 1848, just a few days before the insurrection exploded in the streets of Paris, sanctioned the decrees of the provisional government. According to Article 7: "The right to work is that every man has a right to live by working. Society must provide work to able-bodied men who cannot obtain it otherwise, with all productive and general means available to it and those that will later be organized." And later, in Article 9: "The right to assistance is the right of abandoned children, the disabled, and the old, to receive the means of existing from the state." After those articles setting the principles, Article 132 indicated the application: "The essential guarantees of the right to work are: the freedom itself to work, voluntary association, equality of relations between employer and worker, free education, professional training, institutions of contingency and credit, and the establishment by the state of large public works designed to employ idle arms in case of unemployment." Revolutionary principles were thus reaffirmed and specified. Remarkably, despite the boldness of these expressions, the deputies did not greet them with the general reprobation that could have been expected from the reaction of the country to the June events. Half the offices of the National Assembly admired Marrast's formulations. Between agreement on principles and fears of the consequences of their implementation, positions in the discussion of September 1848 wavered significantly.[35]

The first fear was that the right to work would lead inevitably to socialism, that is, to complete control of the economic system by the state. The objection was that if the state promised work to all those who lacked it for any reason, it would have to give everyone a job corresponding to his qualifications. The state would then become a manufacturer, a merchant, a large or small producer: burdened with all needs, it would inevitably possess a monopoly of all industries or would at least have total control over them. Many took shelter behind these fears to avoid dealing with the basic issue. With rare exceptions, the champions of the right to work also admitted that the issue was not on the agenda. As Ledru-Rollin said: "When you place the right to work on the agenda, you will not have to organize it the next day."[36]

Thiers was the only one who confronted it, advocating a struggle against unemployment while emphatically refusing to recognize the right to work: "I do not think it is impossible that the state can come to the aid of workers in times of unemployment. I think it must reserve certain public works to substitute for private works, when private works are lacking; but all of that is limited, all of that is accidental, all of that is due to schemes that may or may not succeed. . . . It is aid that the state can give and nothing else. It should not be called a right."[37] Yes to a social policy, but no to the recognition of a social right, said Thiers. Priority to the recognition of the social right, even if policies don't follow, replied Ledru-Rollin. The political stake was obvious, for it dealt directly with relations between socialism and democracy, their common origin and their point of separation: was the social revolution of property the natural extension of the revolution of civil rights? But the confrontation also illustrated the difficulty of coming up with a legal formulation of the notion of social right when divorced from the simple statement of social purpose. In 1848, if the right to work was added to the right to assistance, the latter clearly ceased to be a limited right and became a right that reorganized the state and society on new bases.

The basic philosophical debate did not really take place in 1848, when discussion centered on a policy and an experiment of state economic intervention and of the national workshops. And it was the consequences of that intervention, in terms of the state's influence on society, that were feared or accepted: Tocqueville brandished the specter of a trustee state, while Ledru-Rollin put the image of an "intelligent protector state" into context. But the basic problem—of limits—was not resolved. Somehow, it was kept at a distance, reduced to arguments of opportunity or efficiency.

## *The Criticism of the Right*

How can legal assistance to the poor be defined when it is perceived only in the old categories of charity based on compassion? For everyone agreed that an approach of individual charity was no longer sufficient in a democratic society based on civil equality and the recognition of the individual as a subject with rights. However, the liberals often made do with a purely negative conception of the problem, showing the difficulties raised by the notion of a social right to assistance, as represented by Thiers's thinking. How, he commented in 1848, can we speak of a right of assistance to the poor when we recognize implicitly that the application of such a right must be connected to an assessment of the concrete individual situation? A right is necessarily universal, automatic, undifferentiated in its application. As he told the deputies: "You would have to reserve judgment in cases; you must say: I am giving today, I am not giving tomorrow; I am giving in the winter, I am not giving in the summer; I am giving in times of depression, I am not giving in times of prosperity. And you would call that a right, when you remain masters of deciding cases? No, that is not a right, or you have forgotten the language. . . . A right, gentlemen, does not make an exception between classes of citizens, a right applies to everyone."[38] Thiers's reasoning is logically indisputable, but it also has the disadvantage of dissipating the legal vagueness concerning positive right, which is the very problem to be resolved.

Gérando explored another path, trying to work out the distinction between morality and the positive right of assistance in terms that would be constantly adopted in subsequent discussion. Poverty, he explained in substance, has rights. The entitlements of the pauper are within the scope of his misfortune itself. But those rights, while sacred, are only natural rights. The right to life is thus essentially private: it is a moral right and not a positive right, and thus is relatively indeterminate. As Gérando wrote: "There is nothing analogous to the rights of property, the rights of the creditor, the rights born of positive obligations. The right to be helped is not of the same nature as the right to be respected in one's life, liberty, property, honor: although no less sacred, it is less positive, less rigorous, less absolute. It is not the right to request, to demand a benefit, to carry out an activity, to have some advantage or other attributed to one: it is a legitimate hope; it is a powerful recommendation; it is a solicitation worthy of the greatest respect. It is not the claim for a debt; it is the correct expectation of a favor."[39]

Gérando thus tried to settle the issue of the legal status of assistance to the poor by considering it as a moral duty of society, but not as an obligation, which is absolute and strict by nature. Subsequently, all the French liberals were inspired by this analysis to reject the very idea of social rights—of "legal charity," to use the contemporary expression—while recognizing the legitimacy of a system of public charity. Although clear and defensible in principle, such an opposition did not deal with the actual morality of the state and society.

Setting the boundaries of social rights conceived as positive rights is equally impossible within the framework of liberal thought. But rights must then rest on a clearly identifiable claim to be recognized as such. The entitlement on which the right is based falls within a calculation of reciprocity and compensation. Thus. the disabled veteran or the war widow can be said to have a claim on society since they have, in fact, given something for it. Society's debt toward them is legally the same as the indemnity paid to a person dispossessed for public utility. In that sense, liberals always recognized the legitimacy of social-claim rights. But the difficulty is to determine the origin of indisputable claims in a complex society.

While legally relevant, the principle of the claim becomes increasingly difficult to differentiate from simple moral rights in a context of socialization. Practically, it is as fragile as the distinction between moral rights and positive rights.

## *The Past of an Idea*

Although attempted twice, during the French Revolution and then especially in 1848, the shift from passive assistance (the distribution of aid) to active inclusion through work was never taken to its conclusion in Western countries. After 1848, it seemed a parenthesis had been closed. The idea of assistance through work remained present afterward, but only as part of the gamut of interventions used by private charity, pertaining only to a few thousand men and women at the end of the nineteenth century.[40] In 1896, although the Superior Council of Labor estimated that "the creation of work sites for the unemployed is preferable to the distribution of aid in kind or in money,"[41] its wish did not produce any specific public intervention. Even the socialists finally abandoned the right to work, deeming it impossible to implement in the capitalist system. As they saw it, by collectivizing the means of production, socialist society would automatically resolve the issues of assistance and employment, for everyone would be guaranteed a normal living from his work. Thus, they intended to devote all their energies to the revolutionary struggle for socialism. Obviously, they did not neglect protest action in the short term, but in this framework they were content to preach the recourse to big works during bad times.[42]

Ever since the 1930s, the idea of the right to work has progressively been dissolved into the Keynesian perspective of public policies of stimulating the economy, thus transforming the old notion of assistance through work. Roosevelt launched that development by initating a vast public works program, the Works Progress Administration (WPA), designed to employ three million unemployed workers: "The Federal Government," he said, "must and shall quit this business of relief."[43] Although the goals were the same, this was no longer the old model of the charity workshops: henceforth, the creation of jobs for the unemployed was expected to be at public expense and to maintain demand.[44]

The perception of unemployment had changed considerably from another aspect, too. Back in the mid-nineteenth century, the notion of involuntary inactivity was very imprecise; distinctions between the the marginal pauper, the beggar, and the laborer out of work were unclear (hence it was crucial to evaluate the behavior of the poor). The vague and undifferentiated category of poverty, which concealed those different realities, was dissipated at the beginning of the twentieth century, when the modern notion of unemployment (forced inactivity due to a lack of work) gradually emerged. Among the many forms of inactivity, one stands out as independent of the behavior of the individual: the one produced by a malfunction of the labor market on a macroeconomic cause, and specifically defined as "unemployment."[45] William Beveridge expressed that new approach in a work titled, significantly, *Unemployment, a Problem of Industry* (1919). Surprisingly, it was only after 1896 that the French census used the category of "unemployed." Previously, statisticians used vague classifications to describe non-work: "without profession," "profession unknown," "unclassified individual."[46]

The precision of the concept permitted a new approach of social action. Understood as an accident, assimilated into a short-term economic analysis, unemployment could be treated in an insurance framework with contributions deducted from labor. By the same token, unemployment payments could no longer be comparable to any form of assistance: they became a payment due, the equivalent of contributions. In that new context, the previous issue of the relations between a right to assistance and a benefit of work became totally irrelevant, or concerned only the marginal.

On the other hand, the exhaustion of the passive welfare state leads us back to it. We must then reexplore that old universe, but complicating it to give a new and acceptable shape to the type of social contract that can connect work and a right to inclusion.[47]

## CHAPTER 6

# The Inclusive Society

ONE HUNDRED AND FIFTY YEARS after the Revolution of 1848, the right to work has become topical again. Whenever the classic model of insurance indemnification cannot cope with unemployment, and whenever the dangers of compensating unemployment are assessed, the issue can no longer be avoided. Today there is a vague sense that this is the time for a radical change in the approach to employment, that the classic analyses and remedies no longer work. If nothing changes, we shall be unable to prevent the formation of a new underclass, the welfare state will collapse, and exclusion will certainly increase. This is why we must now return to earlier studies of the right to work, and realize that employment and the welfare state can no longer be separated. Rethinking the welfare state primarily implies a new conception of the social management of unemployment.

### *The Narrow Track*

How can the dilemmas of the past be overcome? The passive society of indemnification has certainly reached its limits, but we cannot simply return to the formulas of the eighteenth and nineteenth centuries (charity workshops, workhouses, social supervision of the poor, etc.). Hence, it is tempting to continue separating efficiency concerns and solidarity concerns no matter what the dire consequences. Even those who perceive the perverse effects of this separation often resign themselves to it, for lack of any alternative. Escaping this vicious circle demands moving into a possible middle zone between the logic of indemnification and the guarantee of employment. By trying to structure that zone, we can hope to go beyond the traditional view of social rights.

The trial-and-error attempt to find new relations between employment and the welfare state revolves around the concept of inclusion. It involves several things: the emergence of new bonds between social rights and moral obligations, the experimentation with new forms of public offers of work, merging indemnification and remuneration, and the formation of a middle ground between salaried employment and social activity. Inclusion today does not refer to a precise legal study or an economically determined employment, but rather to a combination of experimental social practices whose common denominator is an attempt to combat exclusion.[1]

We can begin to advance our thinking by analyzing some new social policies and the discussions they stir. In France, the establishment of the RMI (minimum subsistence allowance) constitutes a good example of what might be called the new gray area of the welfare state. In the United States, research is fueled by the debates of the 1980s around the idea of workfare, and the reforms proposed by Bill Clinton in 1993–94.

## The Discreet Revolution of the RMI

Established in 1988, the French RMI is a hybrid, neither assistance nor Social Security, but based on the mutual commitment of the individual and the collective to deal with the needs, aspirations, and possibilities of the beneficiaries.[2] It represents a new type of social right, occupying a middle position between rights and contracts. It is a right in that it is accessible to everyone and recognizes that the excluded should obtain a minimum income to allow them to reenter society; thus it corresponds to a social debt. But it is also a contract insofar as it is linked to an exchange: the beneficiary's commitment to inclusion.

This notion of commitment is imprecise and encompasses diverse acts, such as training, public works in administrations or associations, even simple personal efforts of readjustment (detoxification, for example). However, in all cases, it implies considering individual behavior and the specific situation in the exercise of the right. In this respect, the RMI is a legal paradox, based on an "individualized right." The route of inclusion is adapted to the needs of the person and to the possibilities of inclusion, and depends on the unique situation of each beneficiary. Thus, a fifty-five-year-old widow who does not plan to return to work and is well-integrated into her environment can be offered useful activity in her neighborhood rather than be encouraged to complete a professional training. On the other hand, a younger recipient, before completing such training, may need help for his personal development, the sort currently guaranteed by the specialized public institutions. Another beneficiary may need only a refresher course to be reintegrated permanently on the professional level. Thus, combining an individualized right and a "conditional right," the allocation of the RMI is subject to a supervision of behavior. Under such conditions, is this still a right? In a strictly legal sense, no, for a right is applicable universally and unconditionally. But neither is it a return to the archaic practices of "legal charity."

Still experimental, the RMI is inventing a new relationship of rights. The object of a right is no longer merely an allowance, a "benefit," but rather a general principle of social life that was once clearly recognized, and includes the right to life, to housing, to security, and to many other things. But these rights could not be put into practice and had to remain "formal" rights. Here the RMI breaks new ground by shifting the constraint of rights defined by universality and substituting the search for a practical equivalence of result for an abstract universality of means. It established a norm that recognizes that individuals are in unique situations and must be treated individually in order to achieve genuine equity. In this sense, the RMI goes beyond the classic opposition between formal rights and real rights exposed by Marx, by trying to flesh out a principle of equity that does not mechanically lapse into equality, but which amounts to enriching and expanding equality of opportunity, and thus moving toward what might be called a *procedural right.*

The RMI represents a profound break with the usual approaches to society, establishing a "third type of society,"[3] which belongs neither to the traditional form of *social aid* (which takes responsibility for the marginal, the "social cases" as they arise) nor to the classic style of *social protection* (which mechanically distributes benefits to those "beneficiaries"). But this middle position is still very loose: the policies of the local committees of inclusion are diverse and fluctuating. Practices are still guided by trial and error since there is no clear social philosophy, and they are currently ahead of theory. We must try to catch up, for creating the theory of these new social objects symbolized by the RMI will enable us to rethink the welfare state. Although the United States starts from a very different institutional history—the insurance society has never existed there—current American debates on the future of welfare lead in the same direction.

## The American Debate over Workfare

In 1992, Bill Clinton based his election campaign on the promise "to end welfare as we know it." How can this be done? The proposal was to consider welfare allowances as temporary, and Clinton talked of overcoming the "culture of permanent dependence" that affected many social beneficiaries: in the early 1990s, 80 percent had been receiving subsidies for at least five years, and 65 percent for eight years or more.[4] To achieve that goal, Clinton offered a radical plan: after two years of allowances, able-bodied people would be forced to return to work, either by taking a job in the private sector if one was available, or by performing public service.

Only under these conditions, he argued, could the welfare state become a vehicle of inclusion, allowing individuals to regain their independence and dignity, and cease to be a system of assistance. Thus Clinton approached the idea of "workfare," a term first proposed in the early 1980s by conservatives. Ronald Reagan identified the essential reform of the welfare state with this theme. The basic idea was simple: recipients of public aid had to provide work in exchange. The target population primarily was single persons, particularly women, with dependent children. Many people saw the allowance these women received, AFDC (Aid to Families with Dependent Children), as the symbol of the perverse effects of the American aid system.

In the mid-1980s, Lawrence Mead, an academic Republican, published *Beyond Entitlement. The Social Obligations of Citizenship*, which clearly expressed the new social philosophy accompanying the rise of the idea of workfare.[5] Mead saw the major problem of the welfare state as its permissiveness. Unlike most previous analyses of bureaucratic malfunctioning, he emphasized the moral and social dimension of the crisis of the welfare state: difficulties the poor had in working, maintaining a stable family structure, attending school. Thus he returned to the analyses of nineteenth-century philanthropists who saw poverty as resulting from individual behavior. According to Mead, the error of social programs is that they provide financial aid without any exchange, hence the proposal to link public aid to an obligation to work. Considered in this perspective, workfare was ambiguous, corresponding not so much to a new approach to social rights and inclusion as to a strategy of regulation and control of the poor, particularly the young: "Many young people today, especially at the bottom of society, simply are not as well socialized by adults as they used to be. They cannot be integrated unless they become something closer to the disciplined workers the economy demands. In some form government must take over the socializing role."[6] Lawrence Mead considered putting the beneficiaries of the welfare state to work mainly as moral improvement.

During the 1980s, many American states set up programs geared to that philosophy, such as WIN (the Work Incentive program) in New York, GAIN (Greater Avenues for Independence) in California, etc., but the results were often deceptive.[7] Established in 1986, the California program, for example, had only a limited success: of 650,000 families on welfare in the early 1990s, less than 2000 performed jobs on workfare in exchange for the allowances they received![8] True, the sanctions for nonparticipation were minimal, from $40 to $70 a month in most states, barely an average of 10 percent of allowances; and these sanctions were hardly applied. The strong opposition of the public service employee unions, who feared that workfare would eventually decrease the number of ordinary public jobs, also limited the scope of the experiments. It was hard to make the jobs available for workfare, and political reluctance was also very strong. Democrats considered welfare allowances a right and wanted no obligation imposed on them, even if training and inclusion were offered. All these factors coalesced to limit the scope of the programs.

However, by the end of the 1980s, strong ideological opposition was removed. Although the discussion of means persisted, a consensus on the need to break the culture of dependence was gradually emerging, as expressed by the 1988 adoption of the Family Support Act, marking an important turning point in the approach to society. Henceforth, even the Democrats admitted that work was preferable to welfare.[9] The Family Support Act did not force the recipients of AFDC to work, but it moved toward a demand for training, and granted subsidies to encourage states to take care of children and mothers on welfare in order to promote work for the mothers. While this hardly represents a great upheaval, the law did signal the new credo that the key problem of the welfare state was to reduce the dependence of some persons. A sociological initiative was substituted for a logic of financial aid.[10]

Yet, in the early 1990s, the conservatives avoided workfare, aware that substituting social activities for welfare allowances could produce an extension of state economic intervention, for the state would create its own public jobs to apply the principle of workfare.[11] Thus, Clinton appropriated the conservative programs of the 1980s by proposing a return to work after two years of welfare, and he also broke with the traditional liberal vision of the Democrats. His advisor on welfare, David Ellwood, now sounds like Lawrence Mead in the 1980s, except for the moralism (which is not insignificant).[12] Social rights and economic inclusion are now perceived in new terms, but the reluctance and hesitation have not all been overcome. On the left, some Democrats raise the specter of "slavefare," and social workers are very reserved.[13] But the turning point has certainly been achieved.

Many questions are still not answered and the difficulties of deriving realistic and efficient social measures from a general principle are a long way from resolution. For example, what will happen after the two-year limit on allowances? Will it be necessary to create a new social minimum for those who are excluded from the system because of their behavior? And, on the other hand, isn't there a risk that the first two years will be considered an automatic right prior to any economic inclusion, so that the number of recipients will soar?[14] Moreover, in the summer of 1994, the Clinton administration began weakening its own plan by anticipating exceptions to the two-year rule, allowing the states to exceed that limit in 10 percent of the cases for "good reasons" (another 10 percent exemption was anticipated if an extension of allowances was linked with a training program). Yet with Clinton's proposals something irreversible has clearly taken place in the United States, and the welfare state there has begun its mutation.

## *The Redefinition of Society*

The crisis of the welfare state assumes different forms in the United States and in Europe. In the United States, what is called welfare covers only social assistance, while in Europe the welfare state includes all the mechanisms of social security provided through insurance (national health insurance, old-age pensions, unemployment benefits). Thus, an unemployment allowance is not the same as an AFDC allowance, since unemployment compensation is in exchange for a contribution and is not a social right, in the strict sense. It results from an insurance contract, not from the generosity of the state. This distinction is indisputable, but the border between insurance and assistance is still becoming porous because of rising long-term unemployment and increasing numbers of excluded. In any case, serious problems arise only beyond the insurance phase of indemnification for unemployment, where questions of exclusion and inclusion come up. Hence, the American problematic of workfare will soon become familiar to Europe, and has already started infiltrating practices in some countries. In Sweden, for example, more than half the unemployed are now expected to perform socially useful work in exchange for their indemnity, and Germany is also moving in that direction.

More broadly, the French RMI and the American plans linked to workfare lead remarkably to the same of redefinition of society. These programs have three aspects in common, concerning the relationship between the economic and the social, the nature of social rights, and the definition of the "subjects" of the social. In both cases, the social and the economic spheres seem inseparable, work and the welfare state now overlap. Since neither the market (because of modernization) nor the state (because of the deficit) can create social activities beyond the passive welfare state, a "third sector" must return to the agenda. In the 1970s, it was affiliated with an alternative to nationalization and state control of the economy, but today it assumes a more social dimension, linked to inclusion. In both cases, social rights are reinterpreted as a contract articulating rights and obligations. As we shall see in the next chapter, the welfare state is finally confronted with a genuine revolution of what it represents: it is more and more specific individuals who must be dealt with, and less and less general populations.

*Positive Obligations*

Whatever the precise modalities, we are moving inevitably toward the formulation of exchanges for social rights.[15] Do such obligations constitute a regression to a zero-sum game, in which more constraint necessarily means fewer rights? Possibly, but establishing a new relation of right and obligation can also develop the classical concept of social rights and make it more complex.

For example, the right to inclusion goes much further than a classical social right. First, it enriches that social right with a moral imperative: beyond the right to subsistence, it tries to shape the right to social usefulness, considering individuals as active citizens and not merely those who need help. Thus, inclusion contributes to defining a right of the democratic age, connecting economic aid with social participation. When rights are derived solely from a theory of social debt, they are passive, based on dependency (and were recognized and formulated in a predemocratic age); the beneficiary is inferior. The obligation, however, contributes to resocialization, considering individuals as full members of a society and thus affirming not only the right to live but the *right to live in society*.

Here the obligation is not only on the side of the recipient, it is a positive constraint on society itself, encouraging it to take rights seriously. The path of a *mutual involvement* of the individual and society emerges between traditional social right and paternalistic social aid, equidistant between the passive welfare state that has become too costly and the old discarded society of assistance. Increasing use of contracts in social work reflects this third way, albeit in a still stammering and experimental fashion. As one social worker noted, "The contract establishes a relation of mutuality, giving responsibility to the beneficiary who is considered an actor in his own future, and an obligation to provide means on the part of society."[16] Although he may be in a difficult situation, even in great distress, the subject of social action is considered an autonomous, responsible person, capable of making commitments and honoring them. This practice has been recognized in France by several studies.[17] For example, in social aid to children, the law of June 6, 1984, produced contractual relations between parents and that service for administrative benefits. Similarly, optional aid to adults younger than twenty-one has often led to formulating contracts with them that take their plans into account. The law of July 29, 1992, instituting measures of social action for young people in trouble, also anticipates mutual contracts.

The notion of contract, and hence of positive obligation, is also at the center of the RMI. An administrative circular of March 27, 1993, specified: "The RMI is a right that rests on a *contract* of inclusion based on mutual commitments: that of the interested party who promises to participate in acts or activities of inclusion defined with him, and that of the collective which promises to offer acts and activities of inclusion corresponding to needs." This is not a contract in the sense of a civil right, but, the circular continued, the contract "demonstrates the ability of the beneficiaries to commit themselves and recognizes their dignity as citizens, actors, and not welfare recipients."

The contract of inclusion enriches the solitary confrontation of the individual and society by linking it to the generative principle of society, the social contract. The contract of inclusion has more than a moral or pedagogical value, but must also be given its full legal dimension. Thus, in its own way, inclusion connects right and policy, granting the idea of social right its true dimension.[18] The accompanying obligation is not a restriction of freedom but an instance of constructing society, showing that inclusion forces a radical reconsideration of the organizing principles of the individualist society, and that as long as we remain within a classic individualist scheme, we cannot go beyond the dilemmas of the passive welfare state.[19] Conceived historically, the theory of inclusion also corresponds to a stage of social life where the problem is no longer merely winning rights but making them live as real rights.[20] Obligations can certainly be defined as positive by that standard, allowing a way out of the old sequence of protection and dependence.[21] Moreover, by recalling the history of the security/freedom dilemma, we can get a better measure of the rupture produced by positive obligations in the view of society.

## Security versus Freedom

The modern individual is eager to remove the specter of dependence. During the French Revolution, Saint-Just clearly formulated the imperative for the state: "To give all Frenchmen the means of obtaining the basic necessities of life without depending on anything but the laws and without mutual dependence in the civil state."[22] In his *Rapport sur les moyens d'extirper la mendicité (an II)* (Report on the Means of Eradicating Begging, Year II), Barère also noted that "all dependence between one man and another must be banned in a republic."[23] But was this independence compatible with security? The charitable tradition of the ancien regime associated the exercise of a duty of solidarity with a guardianship of the poor, and social policies were both charitable and policing, responsibility for individuals was necessarily accompanied by control over them.

By stressing the principle of autonomy, modern society comes up against a serious problem of defining an adequate exercise of solidarity, and must devise a non-degrading assistance that takes the form of a right and not a guardianship. Whatever the hazards of his life, the individual intends to remain a full citizen.

To overcome this difficulty, the French revolutionaries of 1789 excluded from the civic sphere all those who were not considered in control of their own will, not fully independent individuals, and thus deprived servants, women, children, and paupers of the right to vote.[24] Moreover, the political rights for the poor came very late. Even in 1873, disenfranchising persons admitted to hospices was considered very seriously, and the municipal law of 1884 reflected these questions, anticipating that recipients of charity could not be elected as municipal councillors.[25] Perhaps this was rearguard legislation, a simple vestige of depriving dependent people of citizenship, but it took a century (1975) before that article was repealed!

In the first half of the nineteenth century, the suffrage qualification kept all paupers away from the ballot box. By the same token, noncitizens could be treated as assisted persons: social dependence went hand in hand with political insignificance. At the same time, political autonomy and economic security were seen as contradictory, a very palpable contradiction in that era. It was generally thought that modern society freed individuals from their previous constraints, but simultaneously made them more vulnerable.

This contradiction was clearly expressed by Baron de Gérando, the author of the great treatise *De la bienfaisance publique* (On Public Charity):

> There is only one state of society in which all access to poverty can be closed off: the one in which—as in the slave system of antiquity, in feudal serfdom, or the guild system, wherever work is subjugated—the lower class of society renounces its independence, and pays that price for its security through the forced protection of its masters, at the price of its moral dignity, and even of a large portion of its material well-being. The poor would then be abolished because there would be no opportunity for adversity or for prosperity. True, members of the proletariat could hope only for what was strictly necessary; but they would generally have the hope of achieving it. Spontaneous work would not exist for them; work would not be necessary for them as a resource; it would be imposed as a yoke, to the full extent that their strength would enable them to work. But as soon as man becomes the arbiter of his own fate, he must suffer the consequences of his errors and his mistakes. As soon as man is emancipated, the use of his freedom exposes him to a thousand accidents. Hence the most critical situation for man is the moment of his emancipation, the move from the condition of servitude or vassalage to the state of complete independence.[26]

The comparison of ancient slavery and the modern proletariat was fundamental for nineteenth-century philanthropists, who perceived the relations between security and freedom as a zero-sum game. As Tanneguy

Duchâtel noted, "With the free contract, no more subjugation on one side, no more duty of protection on the other: the worker gives his labor, the employer pays the wage agreed upon; their mutual obligations are reduced to that. . . . Such is then the inevitable result of freedom of labor: it makes the condition of the workers more precarious."[27]

Although they did not go so far as to claim that the situation of the ancient slave was preferable to that of the modern pauper, several philanthropists did not hesitate to express their nostalgia for the old Roman or medieval guilds.[28] After tracing their history, Moreau-Christophe noted: "It is thanks to this institution, which was no doubt tyrannical, but definitely farsighted, that the working classes of antiquity could resist the causes of dissolution, degradation, and poverty, which so actively obsess the working classes of our own day."[29] The extension and redefinition of the workhouse in England in 1834 expressed this trend perfectly: assistance seemed justifiable only if it deprived its beneficiaries of their autonomy.[30]

Tocqueville had this contradiction in mind when he glimpsed in modern societies the onset of an "immense and tutelary power" that would be the condition of security. More recently, in their own way, "socialist" states instituted a system of social rights without citizenship, embodying a form of welfare state that guaranteed a whole set of material rights in exchange for political subordination.[31] Moreover, this allows a reunderstanding of the contrast between formal rights and real rights, which does not refer merely to the classical criticism of "bourgeois" freedoms. Included in this framework, the Marxist praise of real rights often expresses merely a choice of the "archaic" solution of security as opposed to freedom, thus remaining within the problem and not solving it.

## *The Right to Beg*

The transformation of the legal status of begging and vagrancy reflects the same problem. Until very recently, corresponding to an ancient heritage, begging and vagrancy were considered a crime in most countries.[32] In the seventeenth or eighteenth century, the beggar was accused of seceding from society, of violating the natural order; he was a selfish individual, trying to bend the rules of exchange by refusing to do his duty. Such a view assumes that everyone has his assigned place in the social organism. In a society of constraint, that inclusion could in fact be guaranteed if everyone accepted their places without balking.

Although the individualist revolution cancelled that vision, the view of begging and vagrancy was not changed, so significant was its moralist expression. Only the arguments changed: now the beggar was reproached for not playing the game of individual autonomy, for refusing to enter the age of personal responsibility. On the other hand, since the right to inclusion could not be guaranteed, the crime of begging and vagrancy was almost never prosecuted.

Today, things have been clarified. In France, the new penal code has abolished that crime. In the United States, even if the laws of the original thirteen states continue to mention it, jurisprudence shows a progressive reversal. Paradoxically, begging is now considered a choice: some American jurists even see it as the exercise of a human right![33] In this perspective, human rights can thus become the vehicle of social indifference, for if begging is a right, it is because inclusion is no longer a duty for society. In this case, radical autonomy becomes the exchange for an obliteration of the social contract.

The notion of positive obligation thus arises from the acknowledgement of the impasse produced by a purely individualistic view of society. Yet, without reverting to communitarian utopias fueled by a "holistic" view of society, it points the way to a *contractual individualism* combining respect for the individual with the reconstruction of the social bond. Therefore, the institution of a new welfare state is one of the essential elements to resolve the crisis of modernity, creating a framework to invent new relations between what is "new" in individualism and what is "old" in communitarian society.

### The Economy of Inclusion

If going beyond the passive welfare state includes the redefinition of social rights and the formulation of positive obligations, these have meaning only if they correspond to effective proposals of work. The key to the initiation of a new type of welfare state is that *there are no possible obligations without corresponding jobs*. Unless we confront this issue directly, we remain simply with pious wishes and good intentions.

As we have emphasized at length, the passive welfare state is fueled by the gap between the economy and society, which can be done away with either "from below," by bending society more completely to the logic of the market, or by creating an intermediate economic space. It can no longer be done away with "from above," by simultaneous financing through the reduction of inequalities in labor and a compensatory welfare state.

Since the early 1980s, British and American societies have tried to bend society to the logic of the market. Each individual finds his place more easily in those countries than in Germany or France, but only if he is willing to accept a lower salary. In this case, the absence of a minimum wage allows salaries to be flexible, promoting the creation of unskilled and low-paying jobs that are abolished in economies with a higher level of social protection. Economic inclusion is then paid for with an increasing differentiation of status. Fewer people are excluded from the labor force (as indicated by the low rate of American unemployment), but cracks are beginning to emerge there.[34] The boundary is merely shifted: it is no longer between working people and the unemployed, but cuts across wage status. Economic inclusion and social disinclusion then go together. To conquer unemployment at the cost of a massive increase in poverty is not a solution. In England, we find the archaic model of inclusion through radical heterogeneity (the serf and the lord experienced two separate humanities, but both of them were part of a unified representation of a hierarchical world), with one essential difference: in ancient societies, the social bond was founded on the belief that differences were inherent in the natural order, but this is no longer true in the modern world.[35] Democratic society, on the contrary, is based on the principle of inclusion by equality, by contract. If the conditions of a common *civility* are not combined—as in the United States—individuals must either accept or revolt. Hence the anthropological importance of the criminal economy: criminal inclusion sometimes seems to preserve dignity better than low-level economic inclusion.

On the other hand, policies of economic inclusion in France have been experimentally creating an intermediary economic space for about a decade. In France, these policies fall into four categories: processes facilitating the entry of youth into the labor market, techniques of social rehabilitation and professional readjustment of the excluded, devices allowing the employment of unskilled persons, and measures encouraging the long-term unemployed to return to work.

Processes facilitating the entry of youth into the labor market are the best known, and include a broad range of devices. The major technique of retraining and readjustment is based on job-solidarity contracts. Between 1990 and 1993, about one million persons were employed on job-solidarity contracts (CES). Initiated in 1990 to succeed the TUC (paid community service for unemployed youth), these part-time contracts are designed to encourage the professional inclusion of the unemployed. Half of the funding for the employment-solidarity contracts comes from SMIC (guaranteed minimum wage), and they are made with public organisms or associations for periods ranging from three to twelve months (up to thirty-six months in some special cases). Financially advantageous, these contracts exempt employers from paying employee benefits and assume 65–85 percent of the payment of the beneficiary of a CES by the state. As a result, employment-solidarity contracts constitute at least half the manpower in more than two-thirds of the associations, half of the communes, and one-fourth of the public establishments. Since 1990, the profile of the beneficiaries has advanced appreciably. The portion of young people has thus decreased by half: from 1990 to 1993, it went from 63 percent to 32 percent, notably in favor of those receiving the minimum wage.

Mechanisms allowing the employment of unskilled persons are still being studied. The general idea is to subsidize jobs that would not be cost-effective if they were compensated "normally" (and which have disappeared for that reason). The goal is to make those jobs cost-effective for the employer, mainly by exempting them from social burdens: the wage-earner could thus continue to be compensated by the SMIC, while costing his employer less. Measures of alleviating burdens for businesses that recruit the very long-term unemployed have a similar objective. Social inclusion and economic efficiency thus go hand in hand: the SMIC as a minimum to guarantee a normal inclusion into society is in proportion to the real value of the labor.

Through these various policies, a kind of intermediary economy of social inclusion has been established in France, contributing to erasing the fatal gap between efficient business and the solidarist sphere of the welfare state.[36] But in the process several problems are raised that have not yet been thoroughly explored. First, these policies have already initiated the turn toward positive obligations.[37] To continue to be registered in the ANPE (national employment agency), a training course is required in some cases, even for an employment-solidarity contract. But progress cannot be under the strict form of workfare that requires the state to create all necessary jobs, thus moving from the welfare state to the welfare job, with all the risks that would entail. In any case, it would be impractical to manage the system through social institutions paying unemployment allowances or assistance allowances that might have to impose "sanctions" against individuals who do not fulfill their work obligations.

The solution to these difficulties might be to transfer part of the social allowances (very long-term unemployment, RMI in France, AFDC in the United States) to autonomous *social agencies* that would function as beneficiaries for collective or social services and would pay the unemployed to carry out these tasks. The indemnification of the very long-term unemployed, for instance, would thus have two components (whose proportion might vary over time): an ordinary indemnity on the one hand, and a wage on the other. A system of financial incentive to shift the cursor toward work might also be instituted. Instead of creating centralized quasi-public jobs, a much broader range of activities of a varied nature would thus be developed, and modes of self-employment might also be encouraged within this framework (for one of the major obstacles to the development of an intermediary economy is the sense of personal deprecation linked to some service jobs).[38]

The objective of this book is not to develop technical solutions or to produce the economic theory of this new intermediary economy. For example, it must remain within the noncommercial sector to avoid the pernicious substitution that would be produced by applying employment-solidarity contracts to private enterprise (i.e., that businesses would fire their ordinary employees and replace them with unemployed workers whose employee benefits would be lighter). But the various procedures of inclusion will inevitably lead to the emergence of an economic quasi-sector, even if it is designed not to employ a fixed population. This sector must be a space for resocialization and professional retraining. In less than ten years, employment-solidarity contracts have engendered a new economy of services in France. Going beyond the passive welfare state goes together with the pluralization of the system of production.[39] In the final analysis, a transfer of public expenses would be carried out, but it would be a move from a passive expense (indemnification) to an active expense (payment for new services). At an equal or lower level of compulsory taxes, it will enhance the quality of life for all.

## CHAPTER 7

# The Individualization of Society

OUR SOCIAL MACHINERY has ground to a halt. The welfare state founded in France in 1945 and subsequently developed is no longer a model for the future. Its philosophical and technical foundations have crumbled; its organizing principles and procedures no longer apply; and the traditional conception of social rights can no longer respond to the new challenges of exclusion. Yet, more than the rules, rights, and procedures of the state are at issue. It is also confronted with a sociological revolution. In a word, its "subjects" have changed. The welfare state was well organized to deal with problems of relatively homogeneous populations, of groups or classes, but it must now take responsibility for individuals in their own specific situations.

## *From Populations to Situations*

Historically, the welfare state had three elements: target populations, rules and payments, and specialized social workers. Social progress almost always followed the same tripartite scheme. Initially, a target population was identified (handicapped adults, single-parent families, underage mothers, etc.). This population was then defined statistically, legally, and administratively as an object for public action. Then specific rights and allowances were established. Finally, specialized public officials and social workers guaranteed the management of the system, confirmed the status of those applying for benefits, and thus regulated the appropriate target population. Although this system has long been efficient, it can no longer handle the social problems that are now most urgent. The long-term unemployed and overextended households, for example, do not constitute a group or population in the traditional sense of social policies. Each of these presents special situations, not merely individuals to be pigeonholed properly, but a new type of "social subjects."

Classical statistical approaches do not reveal much about the long-term unemployed, for they cannot be understood with the usual criteria of sex, age, training, income, etc. There is no "typical" long-term unemployed person, as there is, for example, a typical educationally backward child defined in terms of simple criteria such as family structure, nationality, and parents' cultural assets. This approach will not work for the long-term unemployed. A plethora of surveys in recent years all reach the same conclusion: there is no a priori characteristic of the long-time unemployed, who are almost completely shut out of the labor market.[1] For example, even 10 percent of sluggish and untrained elderly women find work in France. Thus, we do not have enough precise knowledge of the risk factors of long-term unemployment or of the opportunities for reemployment of the long-term and very long-term unemployed to justify specific policies based on the usual sociodemographic criteria.[2]

The variables that explain the length of unemployment must be sought on a much finer and more individualized level. Objective characteristics (geographical location, age, sex, qualifications) cannot be separated from more specific biographical variables: previous professional experiences (mobility, type of work contract), family structure, personal psychological history, and so on. It is individual situations and trajectories, and not those of groups or populations, that must be described in order to grasp the nature of long-term unemployment.[3] A good example is a remarkable monograph by Chantal Nicole-Drancourt, who has shown that differences of the path of inclusion do not correlate with the classical factors of age or qualification but with behavioral variables, particularly the attitude toward work.[4] This provides the best explanation of why some assimilate quickly, while others experience unemployment, and many prove to be unstable.

Financially overextended households also demonstrate the changing nature of our comprehension of society. Since 1990, a special procedure has been initiated in France to deal with those households that can no longer pay their bills.[5] In less than three years (up to 1993), 284,000 cases were registered. Here, too, it was soon apparent that there was no common portrait of the overextended household and that the phenomenon did not refer only to populations classically considered as economically or socially vulnerable, such as low-paid employees and the unemployed. The population of "bad debtors" proved to be heterogeneous, including laborers and executives, young and old, rural and urban dwellers. Certain factors (marital status, number of children) certainly seem to increase the frequency of overextension, but no solid typology can be deduced from them. More refined studies, on the other hand, have allowed the identification of different kinds of variables than the sociological ones: variables connected to professional trajectory (number of past employers, number and length of interruptions of work) and childhood problems (dissension between parents, divorce, family financial difficulties, school dropout, number of

brothers and sisters, profession of father at birth, organic and psychoso-
matic illnesses).[6] Once again, the history of individuals is decisive.[7]

### Exclusion: Trajectories and Processes

The long-term unemployed or overextended households are not populations in the traditional sense, nor are they part of a sociological group, as
was emphasized by a recent report of the Economic Advisory Committee.[8]
They only share a biographical profile: an identical series of social or family breakdowns, the same type of professional setbacks. They are linked by
the "forms" of their history, not their socioprofessional characteristics,
and thus they constitute neither a social community nor a statistical
group.

Instead of trying to envision the excluded as a category, we must consider the *processes* of exclusion. The situation of the individuals concerned
must be understood in terms of the breakdowns, setbacks, and failures
they have experienced, by the deviations and differences that mark them
and not ordinary descriptive facts (income, profession, level of training,
etc.). Therefore, "counting" the excluded is no use, for they cannot fit into
a category for social action. Rather, the nature of the trajectories leading
to exclusion must be analyzed as the results of a specific process. Hence the
new importance of precariousness and vulnerablity.[9]

It is difficult to mobilize and represent the excluded because they are
defined first of all by their failures, and hence do not constitute a social
force. They are not the new proletariat of the society of unemployment.
Strictly speaking, they do not have a common interest, and are not an
objective class in the traditional Marxist sense of the term. The excluded
form a "nonclass," the shadow of social malfunction, the result of decom-
position, desocialization in the strongest sense of the term. While society is
constituted positively by the coalescence of individual activity, the fusion
of individual features into average characteristics, exclusion results from
a process of disinclusion.

In extremely varied modes, the phenomena of exclusion are manifesta-
tions of social difference and not of social coalescence. Therefore, exclusion does not constitute a monolithic phenomenon. As the Advisory Committee noted:

> To speak of those manifestations is to highlight the functioning of society in
> relation to those differences: they lead to the ostracizing and the real and
> symbolic nonparticipation of the excluded, the result of a normative ap-
> proach. The concept of exclusion, therefore, represents a particular way of
> recognizing and defining social problems as well as the categories of corre-

sponding populations. In this sense, exclusion is not a new social problem, but rather another way of describing difficulties in establishing solidarities, either of individuals among themselves or of groups in the social whole. To speak of inclusion, then, is to be interested in the various forms of aggregations that exist or are to be promoted.[10]

For the same reason, the excluded are "unrepresentable," since they do not constitute a class that might have its delegates or its spokesmen. Hence there are no unions of the unemployed, and all attempts to transform them into an organized collective force have failed. The traditional idea of representation assumes an implicit sociology, for it is orders, classes, and groups that are represented. The excluded do not constitute an order, a class, or a group. They indicate instead a failure, a flaw of the social fabric. Hence there is a tendency for a population to be obliterated by the problem that defines it. We speak more about poverty than about the poor, more about unemployment than about the unemployed, about exclusion rather than about the excluded. In these cases, social knowledge must be substituted for the classic process of representation.

The establishment of the RMI in France has accompanied an awareness of the limits of public initiatives based on the notion of a target population. Until the early 1980s, the classic assistance and insurance techniques of the welfare state seemed to respond to all situations. If holes appeared in the net of social protection, a special system could be adapted to the relevant population. For example, several prompt social initiatives in the 1970s tried to take responsibility for the so-called underclass, but these neglected groups were often difficult to understand and even more difficult to classify.[11]

Had blocking holes in the network of social protection worked, there would be no need for the RMI. But the RMI emerged because the state and the social workers realized that a growing number of individuals in precarious situations did not fit any of the traditional social categories. A whole group of persons living below a certain income level were not even identified because there were no homogeneous statistics, but also because statistics cannot encompass the nonmonetary criteria that are critical: environment, family status, family solidarity. Thus, many beneficiaries of the RMI never before benefited from social aid. They might be called the impoverished "without cause": neither laid-off, nor handicapped, nor elderly, nor caring for dependent children, they were not reached by the category-specific social policies. Moreover, studies have shown that RMI recipients do not stand out in terms of any classic variables (age, qualification, sex).

In fact, there is no statistical explanation for a specific case of extreme poverty, which is almost always fundamentally a personal history. The establishment of the RMI thus represents a genuine break with the previous logic of intervention, "going beyond the narrow targeting of populations with an oblique treatment of situations and individuals."[12]

## *Deciphering Society*

The vague sense of social ignorance that permeates our societies stems from the fact that exclusion is the major problem at the dawn of the twenty-first century. While we have access to a wealth of statistics, paradoxically we seem less able to make sense of society. It is as if a part of reality were sifting through holes in the tight net of figures produced by various statistical institutions. Although we have increasing information that makes individuals more transparent, society as a whole seems less legible.[13] This paradox can be explained quite simply: the devices to obtain statistical knowledge—lists of items, categories, organizing concepts—are out of sync with reality. These devices, products of the nineteenth century, were designed for a society of classes, compartmentalized, organized hierarchically, of relatively slow mobility. They are no longer adequate to describe current society, or can deal with only a limited part of it.

We still live in a diverse society in which inequalities, even if they are no longer on the same scale as in the past, are quite distinct. But if we consider the central mass of the wage-earning population, a vast middle class also emerged, which is more difficult to grasp. This vague term, middle class, must be clearly understood. The emergence of this class should not be seen only as a banal sociological development, not merely as an expression of a transformation of standards of living engendered by the growth or mutation of a production system linked to the development of services. Although so-called middle-class society corresponds partially to the homogenization of lifestyles and the disintegration of social hierarchies, it is also characterized by a tremendous reorganization of differentiations, which are no longer collective (incomes, qualifications) but are becoming more individualized.

Hence there is a feeling that we are moving from a "hard" differentiation to a "blurry" differentiation, in which "most acts of daily life evade precise codification. Structures reflect either a weakening of norms or an erosion of differences. When difference was only a 'natural' by-product of status, it was sought for itself and the search for it was endless. In that context, behaviors become 'opportunist': everyone adjusts his conduct to circumstances. Events recorded by statistics (acts) then lose their meaning."[14] This phenomenon has been well observed, particularly in the area of consumption.

Traditional statistics that assume the existence of stable differences cannot describe this new, more fragmented and individualistic social universe, whose contours are more fluctuating and unstable. For example, types of consumption no longer characterize a group, but give merely a fleeting and volatile indication, hence social categories can no longer be constructed from the information given by these factors. This is the source of the opacity we sense, since the means of statistical knowledge can no longer help us understand the trends of a society with weaker and more diffuse social energies.

From another perspective, classical socioprofessional categories no longer refer to congealed hierarchies. For example, taking the annual median income in France for the category of "mid-level professions," 21 percent of the managers are below this threshold, while 14 percent of the workers are above it. Income level, cultural assets, and socioprofessional category no longer fit together as clearly, and thus society is less legible.

The economic deregulation and increasing unemployment that marked the 1980s and 1990s have only made it harder to decipher society. We sense that our words are becoming divorced from reality, can no longer be used to define it. The inadequacy of language goes together with the irrelevance of statistics and the time lag of policies. The growing number of failures and breakdowns in social issues masks the break with the well-ordered class society. Hence, the confusion of the sociologist, who is used to counting and classifying to decipher society and make trends legible. The crisis of the social sciences is thus part of the political crisis.

The forms of intervention of the welfare state cannot be defined unless new approaches to social issues emerge. While the cognitive output of the big statistical mechanisms has diminished, it is time to make a new use of the monograph to grasp the texture of society.

Methodology involves all the social sciences. For example, the traditional sociological approach, methodologically linked to intersecting tables of data (which integrated all the operations of collecting and selecting statistical materials) is clearly worn out. Now, the sociologist must coordinate with the historian to understand social trends, while the methods of social history are also questioned. After a phase of statistical enthusiasm, social historians have also discovered the quantitative approaches to be deadends.[15] There is now a new appreciation of biography, as well as a certain rediscovery of prosopography (collection of biographical studies to describe a group or a problem).[16] Maurizio Gribaudi and Alain Blum have encouraged the study of stratification and mobility, writing that "The analysis of the life trajectories of one or several concrete characters has allowed a more refined individualization of the mechanisms of forming social physiognomies and a progression to the construction of less schematic models."[17]

To understand society, we must dismiss Adolphe Quételet's "average man" and Durkheim's "sociological fact" and restore to the data their individual values. The redefinition of the welfare state must also include this cognitive revolution.

## The New "Nannies" of the Subject

If the efficiency of social policies forces us to consider individuals in their particularity, the next question is whether there is a concomitant risk of transforming the welfare state into the management and supervision of behaviors. The consideration of individual characteristics implies that they be evaluated and judged, hence the new approach to society in terms of procedural rights risks reverting to an archaic classification of the poor by their merit.

Local committees governing the RMI sometimes look like nineteenth-century charity offices, distinguishing good from bad paupers.[18] There is a real temptation to supervise the excluded or welfare recipients when their allowances no longer come from insurance. Although a copious literature that suspected the welfare state of normalizing, even "policing," beneficiaries emerged in the mid-1960s, it is only now that the problem is really pertinent, long after that denunciatory literature has disappeared.

This is obvious in the United States, where several social programs aim to exert educational pressure or act directly on the family structure, and there is much talk about "learnfare" and "wedfare." Learnfare programs link allowances to the parents' educational effort. Ever since 1988, allowances in Wisconsin have been reduced if children don't go to school, and ever since 1989 both Ohio and California have offered a supplement to adolescents with dependent children if the parents continue to attend school. Wedfare programs encourage parents to feel responsible for their children or to reconstitute a stable nuclear family. In Wisconsin and New Jersey, supplementary allowances are paid if parents get married, blocked if they have more children.[19] More widespread is the supervision of behavior. In Connecticut, for example, drug addicts who refuse to enter a detoxification treatment have their allowances suspended. In Maryland, payments are reduced by 30 percent when beneficiaries don't pay their rent or don't provide medical care for their children. In Clinton's plan, adolescent mothers would be forced to stay in school to receive allowances and would have to live with their parents or some other responsible adult.[20] Ever since 1994, poor women in Quebec have received a monthly supplement of thirty-seven dollars if they breast-feed their babies (to improve the health of the infants)!

We do not yet know how far such programs can go in social supervision, but a new age of the welfare state can be opened by reviving archaic assistance policies. Moreover, some Americans are talking about a "new paternalism" or a "custodial democracy,"[21] and one of the most fervent advocates of those policies even recognizes frankly that "the implications seem Orwellian."[22] Moreover, the ACLU has sued the United States Department of Health and Human Services for "experiments on humans without their consent," challenging a New Jersey program that suspends allowances for parents who conceive more children while on welfare.[23]

More broadly, we are also witnessing today an overall transformation of the relationship between individuals and social institutions. The courts are affected by the same trend, and the criminal justice system is experiencing a mutation, with the progressive shift from the criminal *act* to the criminal *personality*.[24] Criminal justice also assumes a dimension of guardianship, increasingly prompted to express an opinion on the person beyond the legal personality. These days, judges seldom apply standard sentences, but more individualized ones. The judge is turning into a therapist of the social bond, managing individual autonomy (procedures for supervision), intervening in marital or parental bonds (custody, educational aid, support measures of divorce), and almost governing their effects. The term "social response" sometimes even supplants the sentence. Antoine Garapon referred to these practices as "nannies of the subject"; in American English, we might call them "nannies."[25] The professions of judge and social worker thus converge, both are becoming new nannies of the subject.

Such practices seem to revive old forms of paternalism, but things are not so simple and must be examined carefully. The old and the new are indeed blended in the more individualized approach to society today, a duality manifest in the individual approach and the understanding of rights. The individual has been the historical ground of traditional social work. But in the past, it was the moral individual who was targeted, and thus the most important objective of nineteenth-century social work was the moral rehabilitation of the pauper, by encouraging him to adopt a healthy personal behavior.[26] New social policies, however, target the social individual, aiming at the social impact of individual behavior, and not moral correction. They argue in terms of cost efficiency and not of personal conversion. New social policies are perceived in broader frameworks, governing individual behavior by evoking collective imperatives.[27] For example, the social cost of highway accidents justifies the obligation to wear a seat belt. The control of social security expenses may also risk a future slide toward a "hygienically correct" society that would punish the use of tobacco and alcohol.[28] The effects of tearing the veil of ignorance are felt here, too, since increased knowledge of social interactions produces a more precise measure of individual consequence. This is like restoring responsibility to a central role when the insuring model of society collapses. New social policies can refer to the past and break with the abstract view of social issues that prevailed in the 1960s and 1970s; but even if the old and the new sometimes seem to overlap, they have a different impetus.

The tendency to manage behavior also derives from the more overall approach of social protection imposed in the 1980s. Once the effects of contemporary individualism and the breakdown of the traditional family became overwhelming, it became obvious that the actions of the welfare state had to be coordinated with other systems protecting the individual, including local and family solidarities. The growth of the welfare state was linked in part to the progress of individualism; the less the individual can rely on his relatives, the more he must appeal to the protective power of the state.[29] The increasing instability of the nuclear family and the proliferation of single-parent families thus stretch the demands on the welfare state. Since the resources of the welfare state are limited, the issue is how to recreate those forms of "close social protection" represented primarily by the family. This is what is behind all those measures that come under the term "family preservation" in the United States.[30] Lacking sufficient financial resources, we hope to find a "sociological" solution to the crisis of the welfare state and we dream of a coherent and stable family. The state today is not trying to promote moral values (fidelity, filial piety, etc.), but social forms.

## Rethinking Equality of Opportunity

In the future, more attention will have to be given to individual trajectories. Social institutions have already evolved, as indicated by new policies of the 1980s, although at the risk of producing a new form of social supervision. The use of target populations has proved to be inefficient, and public powers are beginning to understand that we must now think in terms of cross-section policies (to deal concomitantly with various kinds of difficulties that simultaneously concern the same person), and in terms of individualized policies (to deal with the specificity of each case). The turning point came in the early 1990s with the issue of long-term unemployment. The officials of the ANPE (national employment agency) are now aware that they must help a million different persons deal with their personal situation. This is no longer a time to apply standardized measures to an unemployed type or to asssume the existence of an unemployed type.

Beyond social supervision, more individualized treatment of social issues also risks arbitrariness, for if the welfare state is not based on universal measures, dangerous inequalities may appear. Yet the history of the welfare state has been a movement from discretionary assistance to rights, a trend completed in most European countries at the end of the nineteenth century, but not until the 1960s and early 1970s in the United States, where the welfare state was primarily oriented toward assistance.[31] In the early 1960s, some AFDC offices still closed down in the South during the summer, arguing that there was enough work picking cotton for everyone to pay his own way![32] The risk of a return of that attitude with more individualistic handling of social issues cannot be overlooked.

As long as social rights are perceived in traditional legal terms of automatic and unconditional access to allowances, any individualization is a regression. But can the use of procedural rights reconcile social progress and rights?[33] Beyond arithmetical equality, procedural rights argues in terms of equality of treatment. Instead of avoiding the legal issue, which is a source of confusion, we must confront it head-on. The crisis of the welfare state is inseparable from an exhaustion of the classical liberal philosophy of rights. Today, simultaneous redefinitions of the subjects of social action, and of rights, go together. If the new subjects of social action are no longer classes, but individuals in a situation, social action must necessarily offer differentiated aid.

To be fair, the welfare state can no longer merely distribute allowances and administer universal rules. It must become a "service state," giving everyone the specific means to change his direction, overcome a breakdown, anticipate a failure.[34] To that extent, procedural rights merge with the practice of justice.

In the model of procedural rights, equity means equal right to an equivalent treatment. Procedural rights enrich the idea of equality of opportunity by offering equity of opportunity, which is not merely initial compensation for inequalities of nature or fortune, but which aims at permanent restoration of the means to get back on track, to confront hazards outside the scope of the classic insurance model (family events, personal problems, repeated professional setbacks). By being more individualized, social rights can also be expanded and reunderstood positively in terms of social progress, while the best the classical approach can do is lead to a problematic of either the "preservation of gains" or the resigned agreement to their slow erosion.

The development of a procedural right is also a novel relationship between the individual and society. The objective of the classical subjective right, as reformulated by the seventeenth-century theoreticians of natural right, was to construct the individual, constitute his autonomy. And while the object of later social rights was economic, they too were conceived on that model of a subjective right. But this traditional approach to rights is no longer adequate when its object becomes the social relation itself, which is what is at stake in inclusion. The object of the right is not an allowance, but a social relationship that can be encompassed only by a procedural right. Rather than avoiding rights, we are reinventing them, reducing the distance between a formal right and a real right.

The implementation of such a procedural social right assumes systems of recourse or appeal. As long as we remain within the framework of classical social rights, the automatic nature of benefits can be handled mechanically and administratively. A more individualized handling of social issues, which amounts to a juridification of society, is acceptable only if there are guarantees for simple protests. Without going so far as to set up courts, it would be possible to implement representation for "users of society," publicity for the principles of intervention, and speedy appeal. Thus, the individualization of society can avoid a return to an archaic paternalism.

# Rethinking Social Progress

THE FUTURE of the welfare state is not determined in advance but depends to a large extent on the future of democratic life. Its intellectual and moral reconstruction demands not only a radical reevaluation of the social question but also a redefinition of social progress.

Social progress has long been identified simply with the reduction of economic inequalities. Equality will certainly still remain a cardinal value, but in a richer and more complex mode, beyond simple redistribution between income groups. A more demanding view of equality will have to take account of other differences between men and women: generational data, natural handicaps, personal trajectories. This shift to a complex form of equality will have to be accompanied by an expanded approach to equity, beyond a narrow legal view of equal rights or a purely mechanical notion of distribution.

The classic welfare state identified social progress with large collective advances and universal measures. But this is no longer sufficient, for universality can no longer be achieved through general rules or uniform allowances. There is always a moment when the rule becomes inoperative, when we must choose between one person and another, and consider behavior and situations. Social debt is not amortized only through transfers and procedures but must also take the form of an individual duty concerning specific persons. Perhaps we now understand more clearly that the state cannot do everything and that a greater continuity between individual action and collective action must be restored. We must develop a reformism based on the individual, adjusted to the multiplicity of situations, and aimed at granting them adequate means for action and defense.

The classical contrast between the individual and the collective no longer makes sense. Reform of mentalities and reform of structures, individual morality and political imperatives can no longer be separated. The moral obligation of solidarity implies a redefinition of its terms. We can no longer speak abstractly of social rights; we must also experiment with linking rights to positive exchanges to realize the rights of the excluded.

Thus the redefinition of social progress demanded by a new active welfare state raises the question of a new political culture. A renewed practice of solidarity can emerge only from a more profound view of democracy and a lucid redefinition of the reformist idea. The stakes are particularly important for the left, whose future depends on the formulation of a new way of thinking of society. The deterioration of socialism derives almost directly from the philosophical crisis of the welfare state, teaching us that political reconstruction must be accompanied by intellectual reconstruction

# Notes

**INTRODUCTION**

1. I have analyzed their sources in a previous work, *La Crise de l'État-providence*, Paris: Éditions du Seuil, 1981.

**CHAPTER I**

1. See his *Essay de quelques raisonnements nouveaux sur la nature humaine* (1678), quoted in Gaston Grua, *La Justice humaine selon Leibniz*, Paris: PUF, 1956, pp. 336–341. According to Leibniz, the mechanism of compulsory mutual insurance reduces the distance between the ideal social state (governed by distributive justice) and the strict state of law (based on commutative justice).

2. Étienne Clavière, *Prospectus de l'établissement des assurances sur la vie*, reproduced in the first issue of the revue *Risques*, June 1990, p. 128.

3. Ibid., pp. 134–135.

4. His *Plan d'une maison d'association, dans laquelle, au moyen d'une somme très modique, chaque associé s'assurera dans l'état de maladie toutes les sortes de secours qu'on peut désirer* was published in 1754. Piarron de Chamousset became general quartermaster of the hospitals of the royal armies, and published *Mémoire sur les compagnies d'assurances pour la santé* in 1770.

5. *L'Économiste français*, July 9, 1904.

6. François Ewald, *L'État-providence*, Paris: Grasset, 1986.

7. Émile Laurent, *Le Paupérisme et les Associations de prévoyance*, vol. 1, 2nd. ed., Paris, 1865, pp. 89–90. We can also quote the jurist Albert Chaufton, one of the great supporters of French mutual benefits at the end of the nineteenth century, who summed up the development of insurance: "Initially, man thought of insuring his ships against the risks of maritime navigation. Then he insured his houses, his harvest, his wealth of all sorts against the risks of fire. Then as the idea of capital, consequently insurable interest, gradually emerged from the confused notions that obscured it, man understood that he himself is a capital that can be prematurely destroyed by death, that he thus contained an insurable interest within himself: he thought up life insurance, that is, insurance against the premature destruction of human capital. He then understood that if human capital can be destroyed, it can also be condemned to unemployment by illness, disabilities, and old age; and he thought up the idea of insurance against accidents or illnesses and the insurance of incomes. Insurance against premature destruction and the unemployment of human capital is truly popular insurance" (*Les Assurances, leur passé, leur présent, leur avenir*, Paris, 1884, p. 228).

8. Although the liberals feared that such insurance would lead to the neglect of individual foresight, they also realized that, in a system based on individual responsibility, the improvident would come to be a burden on the state. In that case, social insurance could contribute to reducing the cost of collective assistance. This dilemma had been at the heart of the discussions on workers' retirement pensions. See Irène Bourquin, *"Vie ouvrière" und Sozialpolitik: Die Einführung der "Retraites ouvrières" in Frankreich um 1910*, Berne: Peter Lang, 1977.

9. Benoît Malon, *Le Socialisme intégral*, vol. 2, *Des réformes possibles et des moyens pratiques*, Paris, 1891, pp. 162–168.

10. François Ewald, *L'État-providence*, p. 177. See also an excellent article by the same author, "La société assurancielle," *Risques*, no. 1, June 1990.

11. See his article, "L'État," *Le Bien-être universel*, no. 4, March 1851, p. 4. The subject is developed further in his book, *La Politique universelle, décrets de l'avenir*, Paris, 1854 (book 1 is titled, *L'Assurance universelle)*. The concept of insurance allowed Girardin to offer a homogeneous analysis of the external tasks of the state (with its army, it insures against the risk of war) and its internal tasks (with its police, it insures against the risks of disturbance, theft, fraud), its social functions (insuring against the risk of poverty), and its economic functions (insuring against the risks of fire, flood, etc.).

12. Girardin, "L'État," p. 5.

13. See Georges Fréville, *Les Retraites ouvrières*, Paris, 1906. He writes significantly: "The misfortune is, that by talking about old age retirement, we get away from the clear notion of disability and keep coming back to the dream of the idle and gilded old age of the petit bourgeois and the civil servant" (p. 49).

14. See "La dépendance: assistance ou assurance," *Actes des Entretiens de l'assurance*, 13–14 décembre 1993, Paris, 1994.

15. A law concerning dependence insurance has been in effect in Germany since January 1, 1995. While the system has the legal form of a social insurance financed by income deductions (1 percent shared between employers and employees), it does fact amount to a traditional assumption of responsibility by the collective for dependent elderly persons. All employees contribute, while an insuring system would consist of dividing the risk within the affected population, i.e., the aged.

16. See the analyses of Serge Paugam, Jean-Paul Zoyem, and Jean-Michel Charbonnel, "Précarité et risque d'exclusion en France," *Documents du CERC*, no. 109, 1994.

17. See François Drouault, "Philosophie de l'assurance"; and François Ewald, "Responsibilité, solidarité, sécurité," *Risques*, no. 19, April–June 1992.

18. See Claude Gilbert, *La Traitement des catastrophes: entre assurance et solidarité*, Report for the Round Table "Affronter les catastrophes," December 13, 1993.

19. René Saleilles, *Les Accidents de travail et la Responsabilité civile. Essai d'une théorie objective de la responsabilité délictuelle*, Paris, 1897, p. 4.

20. See François Ewald, *Le Problème français des accidents thérapeutiques, enjeux et solutions*, Report to M. Bernard Kouchner, Minister of Health, Paris, September–October 1992. Since the autumn of 1994, there has been discussion about creating in France an additional insurance premium to support a compensation fund for victims of (no fault) medical malpractice, modelled on the compensa-

tion for victims of natural disasters. See Stephen D. Sugarman, "Les projets de réforme de la responsibilité médicale aux États-Unis," *Risques*, no. 16, October–December 1993.

21. Modeled on the compensation funds for victims of terrorism, established a few years earlier.

22. See Daniel Cohen, *Les Gènes de l'espoir. A la découverte du gênome humain*, Paris: Robert Laffont, 1993.

23. See P. Molho-Sabatier, G. Tobelem, and J. Caen, "Facteurs de risque vasculaire: du groupe à l'individu," *Risques*, no. 3, December 1990.

24. Jean Bernard, *C'est de l'homme qu'il s'agit*, Paris: Odile Jacob, 1988, p. 247.

25. In 1945, the Mutual Benefit Plan was thrown into disarray by the creation of Social Security, which threatened to eclipse its role and dilute professional identities in a vast unified system. See the texts quoted by Bernard Gibaud, *De la mutualité à la Sécurité sociale*, Paris: Ed. Ouvrières, 1986. In the framework of Social Security itself, it is striking to note that special departments (miners, railroad workers, EGF [Electricity and Gas Workers of France] employees, etc.) have survived although the 1945 plan was to quickly establish one single department. In the autumn of 1946, socioprofessional private groups were revived (see the speeches of Pierre Laroque, the "father" of French Social Security, collected by Guy Herzlich, *Le Monde*, September 29–30, 1985).

26. As for health insurance contributions, the ceiling on them has been lifted completely since 1984. For a view of the whole process of raising the ceiling, see A. Joubert, "L'assiette des cotisations sociales," *Droit social*, June 1993.

27. For a discussion of the issue of unwarranted burdens, see "La crise du financement du régime général," *Espace social européen*, April 9, 1993; and "L'indispensable clarification," ibid., January 28, 1994.

28. See the excellent discussion of Nicolas Dufourcq, "Sécurité sociale: le mythe de l'assurance," *Droit social*, March 1994.

29. See Rolande Ruellan, "Retraites: l'impossible réforme est-elle achevée?" *Droit social*, December 1993.

30. See Jean-Claude Chesnais, "L'évolution démographique des principaux régimes de retraite en France depuis 1950," *Populations*, no. 6, 1989.

31. On this function of deferment, see the analyses of Jacques Bichot, "Protection sociale: clarifier les idées avant de reformer," *Droit social*, December 1988; and "La comptabilité par génération: un nouvel instrument de la politic budgétaire," *Problèmes économiques*, January 13, 1993.

32. See Denis Kessler and André Masson, eds., *Cycles de vie et Générations*, Paris: Economica, 1984, a pioneering work on the subject; as well as the excellent synthesis of Denis Olivennes, "La societé de transferts," *Le Débat*, March–April 1992; and in the same issue, Jean-Marie Poursin, "L'État-providence en proie au démon démographique."

33. See the data provided by André and Arié Mizrahi, *Débours et Dépenses médicales selon l'âge et le sexe, France, 1970–1980*, Paris: Centre de recherches, d'études et de documentation en économie de la santé, 1985; and their "Les tendances à long terme de la consommation médicale," *Futuribles*, October 1990. Some German studies have produced the same indications; see the table reproduced in *The Economist*, December 18, 1993.

34. See the excellent remarks of Jacques Bichot, "La solidarité professionelle se meurt, vive la solidarité nationale," *Droit social,* January 1991.

35. Christian Saint-Étienne, *Génération sacrifiée: les 20–45 ans,* Paris: Plon, 1993, pp. 8–9.

36. For a good general discussion, see, "Paritarisme, tripartisme, étatisme," *Espace social européen,* December 12, 1993.

37. See Pierre Rosanvallon, *La Crise de l'État-providence,* rev. ed.; and Phillippe Van Parijs, "Assurance, solidarité, équité: les fondements éthiques de l'État-providence," *Cahiers de l'École des sciences philosophiques et religieuses,* no. 12, 1992.

## CHAPTER 2

1. Laurent Bonnevay, speech in the Chamber of Deputies, April 17, 1930.

2. William H. Beveridge, *The Pillars of Security and other War-time Essays and Addresses,* London: 1943, p. 109.

3. Article by Robert Salmon, reproduced in H. Michel and B. Mirkine-Guetzévitch, *Les Idées politiques et social de la Résistance,* Paris, 1954, pp. 376–377.

4. Remarks at the National Constituent Assembly, August 6, 1946. And see the many texts in the same tone quoted in Alain Barjot, *La Sécurité sociale. Son histoire à travers les textes, 1945–1981,* vol. 3, Paris: Association pour l'étude de l'histoire de la Sécurité sociale, 1988.

5. " 'Économie politique,' the *Encyclopédie* of Diderot and d'Alembert," in *Discourse on Political Economy,* trans. Christopher Betts, Oxford: Oxford University Press, 1994, p. 20.

6. See Mona Ozouf, *La Fête révolutionnaire, 1789–1799,* Paris: Gallimard, 1976.

7. See the decrees of November 26, 1792, and May 1793. See the pioneering works of Guy Thuillier, particularly, "Les secours aux parents indigents des défenseurs de la patrie de 1794 à 1796," *Bulletin d'histoire de la Sécurité sociale,* no. 17, January 1988.

8. Reproduced in Guy Thuillier, *Bulletin d'histoire de la Sécurité sociale,* no. 17, January 1988, p. 90.

9. Theda Skocpol, *Protecting Soldiers and Mothers: The Political Origins of Social Policy in the United States,* Cambridge: Harvard University Press, 1992.

10. See Sophie Porthieux, *Assurance-vieillesse: un essai de mesure des écarts entre catégories de salariés,* Paris: Documents of the CERC, January 1992.

11. Commutative justice consists of the equality of ("formal") right. It is based on the principle of reciprocity and corresponds to the maxim "to each according to his due," and refers to the ideal of a "just remuneration," considering that equity is inherent in the fact that everyone receives the equivalent of his contribution (benefits, for example, are considered as the equivalent of contributions). Distributive, or corrective, justice, on the other hand, aims at economic ("real") equality, and is based on the principle of redistribution between rich and poor, and corresponds to the maxim "to each according to his needs." While commutative justice can function without a political intermediary (a principle of con-

tract or insurance), distributive justice implies the intervention of a public agency.

12. A positive definition, because we cannot limit ourselves to the purely negative approach in terms of the reduction of inequalities. If it is no longer sufficient to refer to the "reduction of inequalities," it is because, at some point, it must be based on a theory of equality or of justice if it is to be legitimate.

13. See Marcel Gauchet, *L'Inconscient cérébral*, Paris: Éditions du Seuil, 1992.

14. For Aristotle, justice referred to a problem characterized by the fact that it has no possible theoretical solution (the just is not definable a priori); its solution is always practical, connected with experience. In other words, justice is always a *convention*. In economics, the equivalent of this remark runs through all the theories on the foundations of value. See the stimulating comments of Cornelius Castoriadis, "Valeur, égalité, justice, politique: de Marx à Aristote et d'Aristote à nous," *Textures*, nos. 12–13, 1975.

15. This vision of democratic transparency was also linked to the presupposition of a certain simplicity of the social system. Society was implicitly assumed to be structured in relatively homogeneous interest groups and a centralized collective negotiation could allow all potential conflicts to be handled. The social-democratic model was nourished by that ideal for quite some time, and it was widely implemented in certain Scandinavian countries. See the analyses of Alain Bergounioux and Bernard Manin, *Le Régime social-démocrate*, Paris: PUF, 1989.

16. On the particularly urgent problem of genetic information, see François Ewald and Jean-Pierre Moreau, "Génétique médicale, confidentialité et assurance," *Risques*, no. 18, April–June 1994; and *Genetic Information and Health Insurance* (Report of the Task Force on Genetic Information and Insurance), Washington, D.C., National Center for Human Genome Research, May 1993. It must be emphasized, however, that insurance companies want mainly to protect themselves from the phenomena of antiselection (a mechanism produced by the asymmetry of information between insurers and insured, which, in a heterogeneous population, works to the advantage of the worst risks because of information they alone possess about themselves, and who demand the most of a given insurance contract). All cardiovascular patients, for example, would insure their lives for the maximum if insurance companies did not make them fill out a medical questionnaire.

17. See the classic work by Shelby Steele, *The Content of our Character. A New Vision of Race in America*, New York: St. Martin's Press, 1990. Steele maintains that the permanent use of a rhetoric of victimization to establish the claims and rights of the black community has weakened that community, and has produced individuals who rely more and more on society to change things and less and less on themselves.

18. See Laurence Engel, "Les nouvelles frontières de la responsabilité civile," *Notes de la Fondation Saint-Simon*, February 1993 (reprinted in *Esprit*, June 1993).

19. See chapter 3.

20. This issue of tolerance is the focus of John Rawls's latest book, *Political Liberalism* (New York: Columbia University Press, 1993), which marks a clear variance from his *Theory of Justice*. *Political Liberalism* shows how deeply Rawls's

thought is rooted in the American constitutional experience. His main investigation concerns the conditions of viability of a multicultural society; the essential problem to be resolved, he states, is: "How is it possible that there may exist over time a stable and just society of free and equal citizens profoundly divided by reasonable religious, philosophical, and moral doctrines?" (p. xxv).

21. Significantly, there is talk of a "black nation" or an "Indian nation." See Andrew Hacker, *Two Nations: Black and White, Separate, Hostile, Unequal*, New York: Macmillan, 1992. This is clearly an echo of Benjamin Disraeli's 1845 novel *Sybil or the Two Nations*, in which the rich and the poor in England are described as forming two separate nations.

22. See Alan Cairn and Cynthia Williams, eds., *Constitutionalism, Citizenship and Society in Canada*, Toronto: University of Toronto Press, 1985.

23. Without being based strictly on nationality, the right to social protection is derived from the fact of common life. A decree of the French Constitutional Council, dated August 13, 1993, specifies that "foreigners enjoy rights to social protection when they reside permanently on French territory." See J.-J. Dupeyroux and Xavier Prétot, "Le droit de l'étranger à la protection sociale," *Droit social*, January 1994. But the right to Social Security, based on payment of contributions, must certainly be distinguished from social aid.

24. See Jean-Michel Carrié, "Les distributions alimentaires dans les cités de l'empire romain tardif," *Mélanges de l'École française de Rome (Antiquité)*, vol. 87, 1975.

25. William James, "The Moral Equivalent of War," in *The Writings of William James*, New York: Modern Library, 1968.

26. Michael Walzer, "Socializing the Welfare State," in Amy Gutmann, ed., *Democracy and the Welfare State*, Princeton: Princeton University Press, 1988, p. 17.

27. See Luc Boltanski, *La Souffrance à distance. Morale humanitaire, médias et politique*, Paris: Métailié, 1993.

28. See, for example, Morris Janowitz, *The Reconstruction of Patriotism: Education for Civil Consciousness*, Chicago: University of Chicago Press, 1983. In a different perspective, Mickey Kaus calls for the reinforcement of a "civic liberalism" (which he contrasts with "money liberalism") in *The End of Equality*, New York: Basic Books, 1992.

29. For example, 85 percent of the French state that they are hostile to military conscription and favor a professional army (Louis Harris poll, *Le Figaro*, September 3, 1994). At the same time, an overwhelming majority (89 percent) consider it abnormal that a draftee should take part "in a risky military operation conducted abroad by France."

30. According to the poll cited above, 93 percent of those questioned favored national service (in the police, social work, the environment, etc.), and 80 percent thought it should also be open to women.

## CHAPTER 3

1. On this point, which we do not discuss, see François Stasse, "Comment maîtriser les dépenses de santé?" *Le Debat*, March–April 1994; and the report

*Santé 2010*, drafted by "Prospective du système de santé," Raymond Soubie, Chairman (Commissariat général du Plan, La Documentation française, June 1993).

2. See James O'Connor, *The Fiscal Crisis of the State*, New York: St. Martin's Press, 1973; and Robert Kuttner, *Revolt of the Haves. Tax Rebellion and Hard Times*, New York: Simon and Schuster, 1980.

3. A fund that takes responsibility for old-age benefits that do not come from contributions and are financed by resources obtained by increasing the rate of the CSG.

4. On this point, I am following the pertinent comments of Laurent Caussat, "Retraite et correction des aléas de carrière," *Économie et Statistique*, 1995.

5. Which became the ISF (wealth tax) in 1988 when it was re-created (the IGF had been abolished by the right in 1986).

6. For a technical discussion, see Jean Bensaïd and Éric Desquesses, "La réforme de l'impôt sur le revenu: une mise en perspective," *Économie et Prévision*, nos. 110–111; and Gérard Malabouche, "Le système des prélèvements est moins progressif en France qu'à l'étranger," *Économie et Statistique*, March 1991.

7. Robert Castel, "La déstabilisation de la condition salariale," *Alternatives économiques*, February 1994.

8. See Kevin Phillips, *Boiling Point. Republicans, Democrats, and the Decline of Middle-Class Prosperity*, New York: Random House, 1993; Marvin Kosters and Murray Ross, "A Shrinking Middle Class," *Public Interest*, Winter 1988; E. J. Dionne, *Why Americans Hate Politics*, New York: Simon and Schuster, 1991.

9. Thomas and Mary Edsall, *Chain Reaction. The Impact of Race, Rights, and Taxes on American Politics*, New York: Norton, 1991. One of the Edsalls' central concepts is that of a "top-down coalition," i.e., the coalitions formed by the upper and middle classes aimed at rejecting social programs they alone finance. See also Peter Brown, *Minority Party: Why the Democrats Will Lose in 1992*, New York: Regnery Gateway, 1991.

10. See "Goodbye to the Welfare State. Ten Years of Liberalism Have Transformed New Zealand," *The Independent on Sunday*, March 1994.

11. In his request for advice (July 1945) on a plan of organization of Social Security, Alexandre Parodi, then French minister of labor and social security, noted: "Finding its justification in an elementary care for social justice, Social Security responds to a concern to rid workers of the uncertainty of the future, that uncertainty which creates in them a sense of inferiority and which is the real and profound basis of the class distinction between the wealthy who are sure of themselves and their future, and the workers on whom the threat of poverty constantly weights." (Reproduced in *La Sécurité sociale. Son histoire à travers les textes*, vol. 3, p. 9.)

12. Nicolas Dufourcq, "L'État-providence sélectif," *Notes de la Fondation Saint-Simon*, March 1994, pp. 7–8 (reprinted in *Esprit*, December 1994) is an excellent introduction to the subject.

13. On the leftist defense of universalist policies, as opposed to targeted social policies, see Theda Skocpol, "Sustainable Social Policy: Fighting Poverty without Poverty Programs," *American Prospect*, Winter 1988; and "Targeting within Universalism," in C. Jencks and P. Peterson, eds., *The Urban Underclass*, Washington, D.C.: Brookings Institution, 1991; William Julius Wilson, *The Truly Dis-*

*advantaged*, Chicago: University of Chicago, Press, 1987. For a strictly economic analysis, see Anthony Atkinson, *On Targeting Social Security: Theory and Western Experience with Family Benefits*, London School of Economics, Welfare State Program, Working Paper No. 99, December 1993.

14. See, for example, "The Universal Fallacy," *New Republic*, March 14, 1994; or Irving Kristol, "A demi trop malin," *Commentaire*, no. 64, Winter 1993–1994.

15. Nicolas Durourcq shows very clearly that separation and the general anarchy of social scales produce aberrant curves of marginal rates of assets of available household income, showing serious regressions for certain income brackets (about 180,000 francs of annual income for a household with one child or 320,000 for a household with three children, for example).

16. See Antoine Math, *Sélectivité ou Universalité? Tour de horizon autour de la question de la mise sous condition de ressources des allocations familiales*, Paris: CNAF, 1994.

17. See the calculations of Jean-Jacques Dupeyroux in *Le Monde*, June 16, 1994.

18. Although, even in this case, selectivity would not be easy to manage. For example, a person earning the minimum wage may perceive the specific social aid received by a welfare recipient as unfair.

19. The CSG is deducted at a uniform rate from the total of incomes, whatever their origin.

20. Particularly because it is very difficult to restore to the income tax base half of the French who are exempt from it. Not to mention the more technical discussions on the possibility of instituting a CSG including progressive rates.

21. See the conclusions of the "Perspectives économiques" group, Gérard Maarek, chairman; Paris, Commissariat général du Plan, July 1994 (particularly Chapter 10, "Un financement de la protection sociale plus efficace et moins défavorable à l'emploi").

22. In 1945, it had initially been anticipated that retirees in France would pay a contribution for health insurance; but, in the end, the measure was not implemented since the retirement pensions of the time were considered to low for a form of contribution.

CHAPTER 4

1. See the study published by the CERC, *Précarité et Risque d'exclusion en France*, Paris, 1994.

2. See the data of the CERC study.

3. More broadly, it is estimated today that the essential income of almost 45 percent of the adult residents of metropolitan France depends on social protection (the rank and file of retirement pensions included). See Jean Marmot's introduction to the report *Les Comptes de la Sécurité sociale pour 1993*, Paris: Commission des comptes de la Sécurité sociale, 1994. See also Jean-François Revel, "Le vieux et le neuf en politique," *Le Point*, January 29, 1994.

4. *Étude sur l'emploi*, Paris: OECD, June 1994.

5. See Raymond Boudon, *Effets pervers et Ordre social*, Paris: PUF, 1977.

6. For innovative perspectives, see especially, Robert M. Solow, *The Labor Mar-*

*ket as a Social Institution,* Cambridge: Basic Blackwell, 1990; and Edmund S. Phelps, *Structural Slumps: The Modern Equilibrium Theory of Unemployment, Interest and Assets,* Cambridge: Harvard University Press, 1994. For the French case, see the very stimulating synthesis of Denis Olivennes, "La préférence française pour le chômage," *Notes de la Fondation Saint-Simon,* February 1994.

7. Jean-Paul Fitoussi, "Chômage et contrat social," *Lettre de l'OFCE,* no. 105, June 1992; and "Wage Distribution and Unemployment: the French Experience," *American Economic Review,* May 1994.

8. Berndt Ohman, "A Note on the 'Solidarity Wage Policy' of the Swedish Labor Movement," *Swedish Journal of Economics,* 1969, pp. 198–205; Martin Weitzman, *The Share Economy,* Cambridge: Harvard University Press, 1984. Barbara Wootton published her work *The Social Foundations of Wage Policy* in 1955. Note more broadly that some economists analyze organizations and institutions as "overlapping networks of contracts." On this point, see the stimulating works of Oliver E. Williamson, especially *The Economic Institutions of Capitalism: Firms, Markets, Relational Contracting,* New York: Free Press, 1985.

9. Philippe d'Iribarne, "L'économique et le social: la fin d'un dogme," *Commentaire,* no. 66, Summer 1994.

10. Xavier Gaullier, "La machine à exclure," *Le Débat,* March–April 1992.

11. See the analyses of Robert Boyer, "Justice sociale et performances économiques," in J. Affichard and J.-B. de Foucauld, *Justice sociale et Inégalités,* Paris: Ed. Esprit, 1992.

12. The phenomenon in the United States has been amply described, both in its economic dimension as well as in its political consequences. See particularly Kevin Phillips, *The Politics of Rich and Poor: Wealth and the American Electorate in the Reagan Aftermath,* New York: Random House, 1990; Paul Krugman, "The Right, the Rich and the Facts, Deconstructing the Income Distribution Debate," *American Prospect,* Autumn 1992; S. Danziger and P. Gottschalk, eds., *Uneven Tides, Rising Inequality in America,* New York: Russell Sage Foundation, 1993; Mickey Kaus, *The End of Equality,* New York: Basic Books, 1992.

13. See *Constat de l'évolution récente des revenus en France,* Documents du CERC, July 1992.

14. See Gérard Duthil, "Les politiques salariales en France: la désindexation, source de tensions sociale," *Le Monde,* March 20–21, 1994.

15. See L. Mallet, "La détermination du sureffectif dans l'entreprise: démarche gestionnaire et construction sociale," *Travail et Emploi,* no. 2, 1989. On the other hand, we can emphasize that there are also sociological variables that explain the salaries of the managers. On this point, see two recent works concerning the United States: Derek Bok, *The Cost of Talent: How Executives and Professionals Are Paid and How It Affects America,* Glencoe, Ill.: Free Press, 1994; Graef Crystal, *In Search of Excess: the Overcompensation of American Executives,* New York: Norton, 1991.

16. As Philippe d'Iribarne notes correctly, "The remnants of an 'archaic' society contributed greatly to cushioning the shock provoked by economic upheavals. While the modernizers, who talked loud and strong, spoke only of competition and the elimination of outmoded economic forms, these forms remained widespread. Many businesses, which in fact were mainly sheltered from a competition that was

too severe, continued to maintain outmoded plants, abundant social areas, and related activities of questionable efficiency (from canteens to maintaining lawns). . . . Similarly, the recruitment of young people was not always very particular about immediate efficiency. Thus, in offices, there was no lack of 'gofer' jobs where young people without any special qualification could start making their way" ("L'économique et le social," p. 374). On this point, see also the stimulating work of Bernard Perret and François Roustang, *L'Économie contre la société*, Paris: Éditions du Seuil, 1993.

17. *Les Politiques sociales en faveur des personnes handicapées*, Paris: National Audit Office, November 1993.

18. "The new demands of labor transform producers into disabled persons," notes Xavier Gaullier ("La machine à exclure," p. 176). For a general approach to the problem, see Isabelle Ville and Jean-François Ravaud, "Handicap et stigmatisation," in Gilles Ferreol, ed., *Intégration et Exclusion dans la société française*, Lille: Presses universitaires de Lille, 1993.

19. The term is used by Robert Castel, "La question sociale commence in 1349," in *Le Social aux prises avec l'histoire*, vol. I, *Les Cahiers de la recherche sur le travail social*, no. 16, 1989, p. 17.

20. See Dominique Sicot, "Pays-Bas: l'emploi sous perfusion sociale," *Alternatives économiques*, December 1993; Marie Wierink, "Pays-Bas, la mutation difficile d'un État-providence," *Chronique internationale de l'IRES*, September 1993; Martin du Bois, "Dutch Efforts to Mend Social-Security Net Take Lead in Europe," *Wall Street Journal*, December 1, 1993.

21. See Pierre Belet, "Au pays de la tolérance, les faux invalides sont rois," *Espace social européen*, July 2, 1993.

22. This social use of the category of the handicapped must be distinguished from its political use in the Italian style. In Italy, the number of indemnified disabled went beyond four hundred thousand in 1980 to 1.2 million in 1992, the phenomenon being particularly marked in the South (see D. Variano, "Les faux handicapés, symboles du clientélisme électoral," *Courrier international*, December 9, 1993).

23. For a general treatment, see "Pour ou contre le revenu minimum, l'allocation universelle, le revenu d'existence," *Futuribles*, special issue, February 1994.

24. For a profound economic and philosophical introduction, see Philippe Van Parijs, ed., *Arguing for Basic Income. Ethical Foundations for a Radical Reform*, London: Verso, 1992. We can also note here that, since 1982, the state of Alaska has paid every resident, indiscriminately and unconditionally, an income that can go as high as one thousand dollars a year, financed by income from oil production. Ph. Van Parijs considers that the major scarcity today is jobs: the basic income then appears as a way of distributing the income of jobs.

25. See the calculations of Pierre Riché, *Futuribles*, special issue, February 1994, pp. 31, 39.

26. Ralph Dahrendorf, "A Citizen's Income Would Cut Red Tape," *Financial Times*, January 14, 1994. See also, Claude Gamel, "Les bas salaires dans la pensée libérale. De l'opposition au salaire minimum à son dépassement?" in *Les Bas Salaires et les Effets du salaire minimum*, Paris: L'Harmattan, 1994.

27. See *Futuribles*, special issue, February 1994, p. 31.

28. J.-M. Ferry, "La troisième révolution," *Le Monde des débats*, May 1993.

29. See the apposite remarks of Denis Clerc, "Les pièges du revenu d'existence," *Alternatives économiques*, April 1994; and of André Gorz, "Revenu minimum et citoyenneté. Droit au travail *vs* droit au revenu," *Futuribles*, special issue, February 1994.

30. See *"Managed trade.* La régulation des échanges internationaux" (directed by Jean Peyrelevade), *Notes de la Fondation Saint-Simon*, September 1994.

31. Émile Laurent, *Le Paupérisme et les Associations de prévoyance, op.cit.*, vol. 1, p. 23.

32. See Jacques Donzelot, *L'Invention du social*, Paris: Éd. du Seuil, coll. "Points Essais," 1994.

33. See IFOP (French Institute for Opinion Polls), "Les attentes des Français en matière sociale," *Espace social européen*, April 10, 1992.

## CHAPTER 5

1. See two old syntheses: Édouard Cormouls-Houlès, *L'Assistance par le travail*, Paris, 1910; and Marc Lecoq, *L'Assistance par le travail et les Jardins ouvriers en France*, Paris, 1906.

2. Quoted in Marcel Gauchet, *La Révolution des droits de l'homme*, Paris, Gallimard, 1989, p. 96.

3. Ibid., p. 98.

4. See his amazingly modern proposals in the Constituent Assembly, August 3, 1789 (*Réimpression de l'ancien Moniteur*, vol. 1, pp. 272–276). Along with offering public works to the needy, these "offices of aid and labor" were to act as a sort of employment agency, listing both available manpower and the needs of the economy. Keep in mind that Malouet was a "monarchist" who belonged to the right of the Assembly, which shows that even the most moderate legislators adopted a radical position on the right to work.

5. Boncerf, *De la nécessité*, p. 16.

6. On these workshops of aid, see Alexandre Tuetey, *L'Assistance publique à Paris pendant la Révolution*, 4 vols., Paris, 1895–1897 (a rich documentary collection); and Léon Lallemand, *Histoire de la charité*, vols. 4 and 5, *Les Temps modernes (XVIe–XIXe siècle)* Paris, 1910.

7. The text is in Gaufrès, "L'assistance par le travail sous l'Ancien Regime," *Bulletin de la Société nationale pour l'étude des questions d'assistance*, 1893. For a general view of this kind of measure, see Christian Paultre, *La Répression de la mendicité et du vagabondage en France sous l'Ancien Régime*, Paris, 1906.

8. In 1367, the Paris municipality arranged to force beggars to clean the ditches of the city. Robert Castel notes correctly that "the primary objective of the texts that appear in about 1350 is not to administer aid, but to maintain the traditional organization of work" ("La question sociale commence in 1349," p. 12).

9. See L. Lallemand, *Histoire de la charité*, vol. 1, pp. 185–187.

10. Juan Luis Vivès, *De subventione pauperum* (1525), new ed., Brussels, 1943, p. 203.

11. Ibid., pp. 203–204.

12. See "Utiliser les inutiles," in Philippe Sassier, *Du bon usage des pauvres. Histoire d'un thème politique, xvie–xxe siècle*, Paris: Fayard, 1990.

13. See Robert M. Schwartz, *Policing the Poor in Eighteenth Century France*, Chapel Hill: The University of North Carolina Press, 1988.

14. See his *Instruction pour l'établissement et la régie des ateliers de charité dans les campagnes* of May 2, 1775. In the preamble, Turgot noted: "The King wanted to stop granting funds to various provinces each year to relieve the inhabitants of the poorer cities and countrysides by offering them work, and so His Majesty thought that the surest means of achieving this end was to establish charity workshops in the districts that have suffered the most from the meager harvests and to employ them, either to open new roads or to repair crossroads" (Gustave Schelle, *Œuvres de Turgot et Documents le concernant*, vol. 4, Paris, 1922, pp. 503–504.

15. Abbé Malvaux, *Les Moyens de détruire la mendicité en France, en rendant les mendiants utiles à l'État sans les rendre malheureux*, Paris, 1780, p. 323 (the entire second part of the book, pp. 323–477, is devoted to the need for work).

16. See J.-B. Plaisant, *L'Administration des ateliers de charité 1789–1790*, Paris, 1906; and Alan Forrest, *La Révolution française et les Pauvres*, Paris: Perrin, 1986.

17. La Rochefoucauld-Liancourt, *Plan de travail pour l'extinction de la mendicité*, January 1790, in C. Bloch and A. Tuetey, *Procès-verbaux et Rapports du Comité de mendicité de la Constitutante*, Paris, 1911, p. 317, (my emphasis). In a speech to the Constituant Assembly of May 30, 1790, La Rochefoucauld stressed: "Every man who is useless to society is harmful to it, every individual must work toward the public prosperity by the means that nature has granted him. So, work is a duty to society. Society must demand that this work be carried out" (reprint from *l'Ancien Moniteur* vol. 4, p. 497.)

18. *Premier Rapport du Comité de mendicité* (June 12, 1790) in *Procès-verbaux et Rapports du Comité de mendicité*, p. 327.

19. G. Montaigne, *La Police des Pauvres à Paris* (n.d.), quoted by Sassier, *Du bon usage des pauvres*, p. 114.

20. *Quatrième Rapport du Comité de mendicité* (December 1, 1790) in *Procès-verbaux et Rapports du Comité de mendicité*, pp. 427–428. Remarkably, half a century later, Tocqueville was to develop the same questions in almost the same terms (see his *Memoire sur le paupérisme* of 1835, reproduced in Alexis de Tocqueville, *Œuvres complètes*, vol. 16, *Mélanges*, Paris: Gallimard, 1989).

21. Luc Ferry and Alain Renaut, *Philosophie politique*, vol. 3, *Des Droits de l'homme à l'idée républicaine*, Paris: PUF, 1985.

22. "Fondation," in *Œuvres de Turgot*, vol. 1, p. 590.

23. *Quatrième Rapport du Comité de mendicité*, p. 431.

24. Ibid.

25. Joseph-Marie de Gérando, *De la bienfaisance publique*, vol. 3, Paris, 1839, p. 487.

26. Marcel Lecoq, *L'Assistance par le travail*.

27. Huerne de Pommeuse, *Des colonies agricoles et de leurs avantages*, Paris, 1832.

28. Louis-Napoléon Bonaparte, *Extinction du paupérisme*, Paris, 1844.

29. See, for example, Rainneville, "Du paupérisme: moyens d'y remédier dans les grandes villes par la colonisation d'une partie de la population ouvrière," *L'Écho de la jeune France*, vol. 3, 1836, pp. 253–255.

30. Alban de Villeneuve-Bargemont, *Économie, politique chrétienne, ou Recherches sur la nature et les causes du paupérisme*, vol. 3, Paris, 1834, p. 217.

31. Th. Lestiboudois, L. Reybaud, and de Riancey, *Rapports sur les colonies agricoles de l'Algérie*, Paris, 1851. Note that the minister of the interior then made a total report on the situation of agricultural colonies in various European countries: G. de Lurieu and H. Romand, *Études sur les colonies agricoles de mendiants, jeunes détenus, orphelins et enfants trouvés*, Paris, 1851). Despite their special nature, the agricultural colonies established in Algeria from 1848 to 1850 should also be mentioned. In September 1848, a law called for settling twelve thousand unemployed workers in Algeria. Forty-two villages were built, but since the cost of the operation amounted to almost 30 million francs, the experiment was considered a failure.

32. Émile Thomas, *Histoire des ateliers nationaux*, Paris, 1848, remains the standard work on the subject.

33. François Vidal, *Vivre en travaillant! Projets, voies et moyens des réformes sociales*, Paris, 1848, p. 19.

34. Alphonse de Lamartine, "Du droit au travail et de l'organisation du travail," speech of December 1844 (in Lamartine, *La France parlementaire (1834–1851)*, vol. 4, Paris, 1865, pp. 103–121); Victor Considerant, *Contre M. Arago. Suivi de la Théorie du droit de propriété*, Paris, 1840. "The condition *sine qua non* for the legitimacy of property," wrote Considerant, "is that society recognize the proletariat's right to work" (p. 59). In fact, he considered the right to work as compensation for the abolition of the natural and primitive rights of fishing, hunting, gathering, and pasturing—an abolition produced by the development of property.

35. See *Le Droit au travail à l'Assemblée nationale. Recueil complet de tous les discours prononcés dans cette mémorable discussion*, Paris, 1848.

36. Ibid., p. 123.

37. Ibid., p. 217. In his *Rapport au nom de la Commission de l'assistance et de la prévoyance publiques*, presented to the Assembly on January 26, 1850, Thiers even conceived that the state could create a "Supervision of reserved works" to fight against unemployment during periods of depression; but for him it was merely a measure of economic and social policy and not the implementation of a right. On the debates of those years, see Ferdinand-Dreyfus, *L'Assistance sous la Seconde République (1848–1851)*, Paris, 1907.

38. A. Thiers, speech quoted in *Le Droit au travail*, pp. 215–216.

39. Joseph-Marie de Gérando, *De la bienfaisance publique*, vol. 1, pp. 468–469.

40. See the assessment presented by Ferdinand-Dreyfus, "Assistance par le travail: chiffres et renseignements," *Revue politique et parlementaire*, vol. 5, July 1895.

41. See "Voeu relatif aux travaux de secours contre le chômage," adopted at the meeting of November 1896 by the Superior Council of Labor, *Bulletin de l'Office du travail*, 1897, p. 32.

42. Benoît Malon, for example, proposed the creation of "reserve workshops" or "reserve work sites" (*Le Socialisme intégral*, vol. 2, *Des réformes possibles et des moyens pratiques*, pp. 196–202). Édouard Vaillant often offered the same sort of proposals: on October 25, 1894, he proposed a law for "the reconstitution, extension, and cultivation of the communal agricultural area," and "aiming at the attenuation of the evils of unemployment and poverty by using unemployed workers of the commune for this cultivation."

43. Quoted by Kaus, *The End of Equality*, p. 110.

44. Pierre Saly, *La Politique des grands travaux en France*, New York: Arno Press, 1970.

45. Robert Salais, Nicolas Baverez, and Bénédicte Reynaud, *L'Invention du chômage: histoire et transformation d'une catégorie en France*, Paris: PUF, 1986; Christian Topalov, "Invention du chômage et politiques sociales au début du siècle," *Les Temps modernes*, November–December 1987; John Arthur Garraty, *Unemployment in History. Economic Thought and Public Policy*, New York, Harper and Row, 1978 (especially the excellent chapter 6, "The Discovery of Unemployment").

46. Bénédicte Reynaud-Cressent, "L'émergence de la catégorie de chômeur à la fin du XIXe siècle," *Économie et Statistique*, April 1984. In the United States, a first attempt to measure what was defined as "unvoluntary idleness" was made in Massachusetts in 1878, when misunderstanding of the notion of "unemployment" was reduced by distinguishing persons without work who were *looking for a job* from persons without work in general (see Alexandre Keyssar, *Out of Work. The First Century of Unemployment in Massachusetts*, Cambridge: Cambridge University Press, 1986).

47. Among the rare contemporary reflections trying to renew the question, see Philip Harvey, *Securing the Right to Employment. Social Welfare Policy and the Unemployed in the United States*, Princeton: Princeton University Press, 1989; and Jon Elster, "Is There (or Should There Be) a Right to Work," in Amy Gutmann, ed., *Democracy and the Welfare State*, Princeton: Princeton University Press, 1988.

CHAPTER 6

1. See the special issue, *L'Insertion*, edited by Élie Alfandari, *Revue de droit sanitaire et social*, 1994.

2. Keep in mind that the number of beneficiaries of the RMI approached a million in late 1994.

3. The expression comes from Jacques Donzelot, "Le social du troisième type," in *Face à l'exclusion, le modèle français*, Paris: Éd. Esprit, 1991. But the author especially takes as an example of that "new society" the social policies of the city.

4. See Clinton's programmatic book, *Putting People First* (New York: Times Books, 1992, pp. 164–165, italics original): "We can provide opportunity, demand responsibility, and end welfare as we know it. We can give every American hope for the future. Here's how: Empower people with the education, training, and

child care they need for up to two years, so they can break the cycle of dependency;. . . After two years, *require those who can work to go to work*, either in the private sector or in community service." For an analysis of this subject, see D. Besharov and A. Fowler, "The End of Welfare as We Know It," *Public Interest*, Spring 1993.

5. Lawrence Mead, *Beyond Entitlement: The Social Obligations of Citizenship*, New York: Free Press, 1986. See by the same author, *The New Politics of Poverty. The Nonworking Poor in America*, New York: Basic Books, 1992.

6. Mead, *Beyond Entitlement*, p. 87.

7. See the 1974 suggestions of Mildred Rein, *Work or Welfare?: Factors in the Choice for AFDC Mothers*, New York: Praeger, 1974. On the experiments of the 1980s, see Judith M. Gueron, "Reforming Welfare with Work," *Public Welfare*, Autumn 1987; Lawrence Mead, "Expectations and Welfare Work: WIN in New York State," *Polity*, Winter 1985; Michael Morris and John Williamson, "Workfare: The Poverty/Dependence Tradeoff," *Social Policy*, Summer 1987; David Swoap, "Broad Support Buoys California's GAIN," *Public Welfare*, Winter 1986.

8. See the data provided by Michael Wiseman, "How Workfare Really Works," *Public Interest*, Autumn 1987; and Robert Rector, "Welfare Reform, Dependency Reduction, and Labor Market Entry," *Journal of Labor Research*, Summer 1993.

9. On the Democratic turning point, see *A New Social Contract: Rethinking the Nature and Purpose of Public Assistance*, Report of the Task Force on Poverty and Welfare submitted to Governor Mario Cuomo, State of New York, December 1986.

10. The connections between the welfare state and family structures have been fundamental in the United States since the 1965 publication of the Moynihan Report on the black family. See David T. Ellwood, *Poor Support. Poverty in the American Family*, New York: Basic Books, 1988; Daniel P. Moynihan, "How the Great Society Destroyed the American Family," *Public Interest*, Summer 1992; George Gilder, "Welfare's New Consensus: the Collapse of the American Family," *Public Interest*, Autumn 1987; William Julius Wilson and Kathryn Neckerman, "Poverty and Family Structure: the Widening Gap between Evidence and Public Policy Issues," in S. Danziger and D. Veinberg, *Fighting Poverty: What Works and What Doesn't*, Cambridge: Harvard University Press, 1986.

11. See Mickey Kaus, "The Right Abandons Workfare," *New Republic*, February 21, 1994. Ever since then, conservatives have emphasized the need to reconstitute the family fabric and to fight against illegitimate births to resolve the problems of the welfare state.

12. On the new Democratic philosophy of the welfare state, see Laurence E. Lynn, "Ending Welfare Reform as We Know It," *American Prospect*, Autumn 1993.

13. The expression is a significant indication of the difficulty of going beyond the dilemmas of the past.

14. See Christopher Jencks, "Can We Put a Time Limit on Welfare?" *American Prospect*, Autumn 1992; and Mickey Kaus, "A Promising Start on Welfare Reform," *New Republic*, April 25, 1994.

15. For an initial approach to the issue, see Baruch Brody, "Work Requirements and Welfare Rights," in Peter Brown, ed., *Income Support: Conceptual and Policy Issues*, Rowman: Maryland Studies in Public Philosophy, 1981; Robert K. Fullinwider, "Citizenship and Welfare," in Gutmann, *Democracy and the Welfare State*.

16. Quoted by Antoine Garapon, "La déontologie du travailleur social," *Revue de droit sanitaire et social*, October–December 1993.

17. See Marie-Colette Lalire, "Les nouvelles fonctions des travailleurs sociaux," *Revue de droit sanitaire et social*, October–December 1993.

18. But here we do not mean the notion of social right in Georges Gurvitch's sense (*L'Idée du droit social*, Paris, 1931). For Gurvitch, in fact, the term social right indicates the original, non-state-controlled right worked out by social collectives (the collective agreements of work, for example). By social right, we mean the societal dimension that enriches the perspective of objective rights (marking an interpenetration of the "just" and the "good," to use other terms).

19. Here, we must certainly distinguish the American perspective from the situation of the continental European countries. The American problem is precisely that social progress is expressed only in the language of rights (a whole part of the left thus militates for the formulation of an Economic Bill of Rights). By the same token, that country succeeds less than other places in getting out of the vacillation between the passive welfare state and the moralizing management of the poor.

20. See the investigation of Sabine Chalvon-Demersay, *Mille Scénarios. Une enquête sur l'imagination en temps de crise*, Paris: Métailié, 1994.

21. According to a SOFRES poll published in *Le Figaro* in July 1994, 78 percent of the French said they were "rather favorable" to accompanying the payment of the RMI with an obligation to work (for example, for the local collectives), 17 percent were against that measure (only 5 percent had no opinion on the subject, an exceptionally low rate).

22. Saint-Just, *Fragments d'institutions républicaines*, in *Œuvres complètes de Saint-Just*, Paris: Gérard Lebovici, 1984, p. 969.

23. Barère, *Premier Rapport fait au nom du Comité de salut public sure les moyens d'extirper la mendicité dans les campagnes, et sur les secours que doit accorder la République aux citoyens indigents*, Paris: 22 floréal an II, p. 3.

24. See Pierre Rosanvallon, *Le Sacre du citoyen. Histoire du suffrage universel en France*, Paris: Gallimard, 1992.

25. The number of persons concerned was far from negligible. In 1883, 1,405,500 poor people assisted by the charity offices were listed. See Jean Bardoux, *Vagabonds et Mendiants devant la Loi*, Paris, 1906; and Jules Baby, *Le Statut de l'indigence*, Toulouse, 1910.

26. Joseph-Marie de Gérando, *De la bienfaisance publique*, vol. 1, pp. 165–167.

27. Tanneguy Duchâtel, *La Charité dans ses rapports avec l'état moral et le bien-être des classes inférieures de la société*, Paris, 1829, p. 343.

28. However, the Roman philosopher Libanius was often quoted in this period: "Slavery is not at all like the poverty of the poor; the slave rests easy, is fed by the cares of his master, while the poor free man stays awake all night to earn his living, suffering the poverty that exhausts him with hunger" (quoted, for example, by

L.-M. Moreau-Christophe, *Du problème de la misère et de sa soluution chez les peuples anciens et modernes*, vol. 2, Paris, 1851, pp. 145–146).

29. L.-M. Moreau-Christophe, *Du droit a l'oisiveté et de l'organisation du travail servile dans les républiques grecques et romaines*, Paris, 1849, p. 309.

30. See Margaret Ann Crowther, *The Workhouse System, 1834–1929. The History of an English Institution*, London, 1981; and Felix Driver, *Power and Pauperism. The Workhouse System, 1834–1884*, Cambridge: Cambridge University Press, 1993.

31. See Laurence Lombart and Raphaël Tresmontant, "Réinventer la protection sociale en Europe de l'Est," *Futuribles*, July–August, 1993; Xavier Gaullier speaks of "social rights without citizenship that were dependent on the paternalistic arbitrariness of the Party state," *Revue française des affaires sociale*, January–March, 1992, p. 4.

32. In France, see the former articles 269 and 270 of the Penal Code (in effect until 1994): "Vagrancy is a crime. Vagabonds or vagrants are those who have no fixed residence or means of subsistance and who usually practice no trade or profession."

33. See, for example, Helen Hershkoff and Adam Cohen, "Begging to Differ: the First Amendment and the Right to Beg," *Harvard Law Review*, vol. 104, 1991.

34. Although the low rate of American unemployment is also connected with phenomena of voluntary retirement, for the long-term unemployed do not want to be registered for unemployment since they perceive no more benefits.

35. In England, the Low Pay Network showed that lowering wages did not even create jobs in sectors like restaurants and hotels. Yet, we currently find low wages of two pounds an hour in those sectors! For the discussion of the institution of a minimum wage that ensues from these kinds of facts, see "A National Minimum Wage," *The Economist*, September 3, 1994.

36. On this point, where the literature is very abundant, see Bernard Eme and Jean-Louis Laville, *Cohésion sociale et Emploi*, Paris: Desclée de Brouwer, 1994.

37. For a strictly economic analysis of the efficiency of these positive obligations, see T. Besley and S. Coate, "Workfare versus Welfare: Incentive Arguments for Work Requirements in Poverty-Alleviation Programs," *American Economic Review*, March 1992.

38. See Steven Balkin, *Self-Employment for Low-Income People*, New York: Praeger, 1989; and the feature, "Working for Yourself," *The Economist*, August 29, 1992.

39. Thus we do not understand why the experiments of inclusion have not been supported by the public powers in France.


CHAPTER 7


1. Didier Demazière, *Le Chômage en crise? La négociation des identités des chômeurs de longue durée*, Lille: Presses universitaires de Lille, 1992.

2. Raphaël Tresmontant, "Chômage: les chances d'en sortir," *Economie et Statistique*, March 1991; and Mireille Elbaum, "Pour une autre politique de traitement du chômage," *Esprit*, August–September 1994.

3. We can quote Schumpeter's metaphor of the bus concerning social classes: "Social classes are like buses whose route constitutes a specific object of description, even if, on arrival, the vehicles no longer contain the same passengers as on departure, even if, at the end of line, none of those who boarded it" (quoted by Jean-Claude Passeron in, "Biographies, flux, itinéraires, trajectoires," *Revue française de sociologie*, vol. 31, 1989).

4. Chantal Nicole-Drancourt, *L'Insertion professionelle des jeunes*, Paris: CNRS-INSEE, 1991; and "L'idée de précarité revisitée," *Travail et Emploi*, 1992, which notes that, to perceive precariousness coherently, "the trajectory [of the young people] must be considered in its totality and in a very long term to give meaning to events. . . . Placed in perspective in a longitudinal approach, biographical events coalesce to form totalities that present regularities" (p. 63).

5. The Neiertz law of December 31, 1989, established ad hoc departmental committees in the offices of the Bank of France, intended to invite debtors and creditors to come to an understanding.

6. See the pioneering work of Georges Menahem, "Problèmes familiaux, trajectoires professionnelles et incidents de paiement. La stimulation probabiliste du développment d'un *credit-scoring*," in *Rapport au Conseil national de crédit: l'endettement des ménages*, Paris, 1989.

7. The bank grids of credit-scoring, intended to measure the risks in granting loans, increasingly try to integrate such biographical elements. But the collection of such information is currently strictly restrained in France by the Committee on Information and Freedom, demonstrating that the protection of private life can also lead to limiting the studies of social trajectories.

8. *Exclus et Exclusions: connaître les populations, comprendre les processus*. Rapport du groupe technique quantitatif sur la prospective de l'exclusion, chaired by Philippe Nasse, Commissariat général du Plan, Paris, January 1992.

9. See the last report published by the CERC, *Précarité et Risque d'exclusion en France* (Paris: La Documentation française, 1993), which notes, for example, that 37 percent of wage-earners assess their job as more or less unstable. See also the analyses of Robert Castel, "De l'exclusion comme état à la vulnérablité comme processus," in Joëlle Affichard and Jean-Baptiste de Foucauld, *Justice sociale et Inégalités*, Paris: Éd. Esprit, 1992.

10. Report of Philippe Nasse, quoted above in *Exclus et Exclusions*, p. 1.

11. Jean-Michel Belorgey, *La Gauche et les Pauvres*, Paris: Syros-Alternatives, 1987.

12. See the excellent comments of Robert Castel and Jean-François Laé, "La diagonale du pauvre," in *Le Revenu minimum de l'insertion, une dette sociale*, Paris: L'Harmattan, 1992. And *Rapport de la Commission nationale d'évaluation du RMI*, presented by Pierre Vanlerenberghe, Paris: La Documentation française, 1992.

13. Tearing the veil of ignorance, which we discussed earlier, operates at this level of individual situations. It does not mean that social mechanisms become more legible. The two orders of knowledge are separate.

14. Maurice Comte, "Le flou et le dur" in "La cité des chiffres ou l'illusion des statistiques," *Autrement*, September 1992, pp. 161–162.

15. See the stimulating article by Maurizio Gribaudi and Alain Blum, "Des catégories aux liens individuels: l'analyse statistique de l'espace social," *Annales ESC*, November–December 1990.

16. See Giovanni Levi, "Les usages de la biographie," *Annales ESC*, November–December 1989. For the report of the return to biography and microhistory, see Jacques Revel's preface, "L'histoire au ras du sol," in Giovanni Levi, *Le Pouvoir au village*, Paris: Gallimard, 1986.

17. Gribaudi and Blum, "Des categories," p. 1367.

18. Isabelle Astier, "Chronique d'une commission locale d'insertion," in Donzelot, ed., *Face à l'exclusion*. I am also basing this assessment on my own participation in a local committee of inclusion.

19. See the well-documented feature in *New York Times*, March 1, 1994: "Workfare, Learnfare, Wedfare."

20. The plan also insists on parental responsibility and contemplates asking hospitals to determine paternity at the time of each birth.

21. Charles Murray, "The Coming of Custodial Democracy," *Commentary*, September 1988.

22. Mead, *Beyond Entitlement*, p. 87.

23. Dante Ramos, "Rats: Welfare Reform and Human Experimentation," *New Republic*, August 8, 1994.

24. I refer to the works of Antoine Garapon, secretary-general of the Institut des hautes études judiciares; see, especially, his articles, "Le sujet de droit," *Revue interdisciplinaire d'études juridiques*, no. 31, 1993; and "Pour une nouvelle intelligence de la peine" (forthcoming).

25. In the 1990s, this magistrature of the subject represented more than half the activity of the legal justice system in France. What is called "identity crimes" (drugs, family problems, foreigners in illegal situations, etc.) assume an increasing importance in relation to classically criminal acts.

26. See, for example, Joseph-Marie de Gérando, *Le Visiteur du pauvre*, 3rd ed., Paris, 1826.

27. See James Q. Wilson, "The Rediscovery of Character: Private Virtue and Public Policy," *Public Interest*, Autumn 1985.

28. Why not go as far as supervision of food, since that is a basic factor of health?

29. Recall Durkheim's famous analyses explaining that "individualism has walked at the same pace as statism" (see particularly the preface to the second edition of *De la division du travail social*).

30. I have borrowed this term from Robert Castel. See his article, "De l'indigence à l'exclusion, la désaffiliation," in Jacques Donzelot, ed., *Face à l'exclusion*. Keep in n.ind that, in several cases, national solidarity is considered a simple substitute for family solidarity. Thus, the law anticipates that the allowances of the National Fund of Solidarity (FNS) can be recovered from debtors or heirs.

31. Michael Sosin, "Legal Rights and Welfare Change, 1960–1980," in Sheldon H. Danziger and Daniel H. Veinberg, *Fighting Poverty, What Works and What Doesn't*, Cambridge: Harvard University Press, 1986.

32. Quoted by Frances Fox Piven and Richard A. Cloward, *Regulating the Poor: The Functions of Public Welfare*, New York: Pantheon Books, 1971, which analyzes those practices. See also Michael B. Katz, *In the Shadow of the Poorhouse. A Social History of Welfare in America*, New York: Basic Books, 1986.

33. See the discussion concerning Habermas's analysis, referring, for example, to Jacques Lenoble and A. Berten, *Dire la norme. Droit, politique et énonciation*, Paris and Brussels: LGDJ and Story Scientia, 1990. Note that the procedural term is not used here in the same sense as in Rawls.

34. I have borrowed this term from François Ivernel (see his article in *Le Monde*, March 10, 1993).

# Index